Tales from Delaware Bay

JAMES MILTON HANNA

Tales from Delaware Bay
James Milton Hanna
Copyright 2000

All rights reserved. No part of this publication may be reproduced or transmitted in any form or means without written permission of the publisher

Reprinted 2001
Reprinted 2003
Reprinted 2008

ISBN 0-9640458-2-6

Library of Congress Catalog Card No. 99 097 801

Library of Congress Cataloging in Publication Data
Tales from Delaware Bay
  Incidents occurring on the Bay, Commercial Fishing, Boating and Crabbing. True life adventures of people who earn their livelihood from the Bay. Recreational boating and fishing. Muskrat trapping in the marshes abutting the Bay.

Other Books By Author

Cornbread and Beans for Breakfast
A Possum in Every Pot
Beyond Yonder Ridge
The Labrador Saga
A Man Called Shiloh
Southern Tales
Once Upon a Time in the South
Milton's Guide to Self-Publishing and Marketing
Tales from Delaware Bay
More Tales from Delaware Bay
Meandering Around Delaware Bay
Musings from the Bay
Dogs I Have Known

Cherokee Books
P.O. Box 463
Little Creek, DE 19961

www.cherokeebooks.com

Dedicated to:

Herman Moore who helped the author get started crabbing.

Eugene Short who told many stories of working on the bay,

Richard (Dicky) Short whose consistent effort in working the bay impressed the author,

Sammy Dodge who was a character in his own right.

And to

Those who still work on the bay, may all the crabs you catch be "Jimmys" and may there be buyers lined up to purchase your catch at the end of the day.

HERMAN MOORE worked the bay as a crabber and commercial fisherman for many years until he died in 1987 at the age of seventy-nine. He is remembered and highly respected by those who knew him. His sons, Don and Bob, continue to follow in his footsteps and successfully crab and fish on Delaware Bay. Mr. Moore constructed crab pots to sell to other crabbers. Also he supplied paint, zincs, rope, floats and other crabbing accessories.

The author purchased his first crab pots from Mr. Moore in 1969. He asked for and received excellent advise from this older man who had worked the bay since a young man. Once Mr. Moore was asked why he had selected black for a color identifying the floats required to mark his crab pots. He replied in his deep voice, "anything left in Delaware Bay for any time will eventually turn black, and I will not have to paint my floats too often."

Herman Moore has gone to his reward, but his presence remains. He will be remembered and esteemed by those who knew and worked the bay with him.

Acknowledgments

The author gratefully acknowledges the contributions of the following people:

Wayne (Big Daddy) Mills for his congenial help in locating pictures of bay scenes.

Wayne (Herb) Mills arranging for the author to observe crabbers working the bay.

Jack Evans, skipper of the 3 Jacks, for allowing the author to "work the bay" as an observer for a day.

Ronald L. "Boe" Virdin, skipper of the "Miss Barb" for an interesting day crabbing on the bay.

Nora Howell for her illustrations.

Shirley Gelb, outstanding wildlife photographer.

My wife, Frances who encouraged the writing of this book.

Introduction

Foreword 9
Introduction 11

Chapter 1
    Delaware Bay 13

Chapter 2
    The Net Fisherman 19

Chapter 3
    The Anchorage Area 30

Chapter 4
    The Hook Incident 36

Chapter 5
    Sharks 41

Chapter 6
    Crabbing 51

Chapter 7
    Woodland Beach 72

Chapter 8
    Stories from the Bay 77

Chapter 9
    The New Boat 90

Chapter 10
    A Just Reward 107

Chapter 11
    Overnight on the Bay 112

Chapter 12
    Trapping 119

Chapter 13
    The Trapped Trapper 129

Chapter 14
    Meandering 133

Old Port Mahon Lighthouse

The old lighthouse was used during the early 1900s to mark the shallows. It became obsolete many years ago. The building was used by many sports fishermen and watermen as a navigational aid when returning to Port Mahon from out in the bay. (Since this picture was taken, it was burnt down by vandals.)

Foreword

The Delaware Bay is a unique body of water. The people who work the bay for a living are to be admired for their forbearance. Working on the bay is difficult at best, yet there is something that attracts people to the bay like a magnet. The bay lures crabbers, commercial and sports fishermen, eel trappers, oystermen and recreation boaters. One can drive to a boat launching ramp and see boats coming and going from the bay. Just watching the boaters inspires many persons to acquire their own boat and join those on the bay. Seeing the crab boats traveling back and forth tending crab pots is a wonderful sight to view.

Delaware Bay is filled with treasure. That treasure is its resources! It is unbelievable the number of fish and crabs that are taken from the bay. The work is hard, yet people work their entire lives toiling from a rocking boat to harvest the treasure of Delaware Bay. Many people in these modern times enjoy crabs and fish, yet have no idea of the time and effort used to bring these prized morsels to the table.

The marshes bordering the bay are a breeding ground for various species of animal life, including vast swarms of insects. Goose and duck hunting draws sportsmen from all over. Seeing huge flocks of geese flying in the early morning is an inspiring sight. Many people are in goose and duck blinds before daylight with the anticipation of attracting and bagging a few of the evasive birds. In other areas of the marsh trappers are checking their traps in expectation of a good catch of muskrats and raccoon. Both hunter and trapper share the marshes and experience the same exposure to wind and cold, and the thrill of participating in an age old occupation.

Not to be outdone are the bird watchers who are attracted to the many species of bird life that frequent the shore of the bay. Bird watchers come from all areas of the country to view the marvelous congregating of birds, many in transit to the Arctic or to South America. Many of the shore birds feed on the eggs of the Horseshoe crab which cover the shore of the bay during the summer months.

Working the water is more than an occupation, it requires a love for the outdoors and the independence to be found when working for oneself. There are many people who fit into that category of free spirited people. Such people are fast becoming rare in this computer/space age.

James Hanna
2000

Introduction

The author crabbed and fished commercially for five years on the Delaware Bay. He treasures the experience gained from working the bay. This book only covers a few of the incidents he experienced or knew to have occurred while on the bay. He apologizes for not mentioning dozens of individuals by name whom he met during that time. A profound thanks goes out to those who made this book possible. Perhaps my next book will recognize your accomplishments.

I have met many young men who still dream of owning their own boats and becoming full time watermen. Many work or have worked on crab boats. Some abide their time working at other jobs while attempting to save the money needed to buy and outfit a boat for crabbing. They are young men whose goal is to be their own boss, answering to themselves only. I wish them success in realizing their dream.

The real names of persons in some of these stories are fiction. I felt that because of the nature of some stories it would be best to conceal the identity of those involved. Many of my stories involve local people whose real name is concealed for obvious reasons.

Hanna

CHAPTER 1

Delaware Bay

There still exists a unique breed of men who attempt to earn their living in part from the Delaware Bay. Many are following the occupations of their forefathers. These men seek eel, net fish, catch the Blue Crab in wire basket traps, and in the winter trap muskrats from the many marshes surrounding the waters of the bay.

All of this is accomplished on or near one of the roughest inland bays in the world. A place where the waves can go from a dead calm to four to six feet in a matter of a few minutes.

A good waterman—a term used to describe a person who attempts to earn a living from the water—often scrutinize the horizon whenever he is working on the bay. Storms tend to follow the bay, especially in the spring and early summer. To be caught out on the bay in a severe thunder and lighting storm is no picnic. Especially, when there is a strong wind accompanying the storm.

Delaware Bay is dangerous because there are few places where shelter can be found during a sudden storm. There are numerous tidal mud flats where at low tide it is impossible to reach ashore. A good waterman soon becomes weather wise.

The only way of finding a safe haven from a storm on the Delaware Day is to follow a creek or river inland. There are occasions when a boat has to anchor and ride out a storm. This experience can be nerve wrecking. Such a storm occurred in the early seventies. Many boats were caught in that storm, mostly sports fishermen, and the only safe thing to do was anchor with as long a rope as possible. That particular storm created twelve foot waves. Those who spent the night riding out the storm were terrified. Surprisingly, only two people lost their lives. It was an experience that those caught in the storm will never forget.

The watermen are still somewhat clannish. There is a resentfulness of new watermen until they can prove their merit. Often watermen will pass newcomers on the water with nothing more than a nod of the head. Most tend to their own business and expect others to do the same.

Delaware Bay

Several Crabbers and Fisherman once operated from the Little Creek Docks. Richard (Dickie) Short worked out of this area for several years. Dickie died a few years ago. He was a good man and is missed by those who worked the bay with him.

A Good Place To Buy Seafood

The fish market in Little Creek, Delaware sells fish and crabs fresh from the waters of Delaware Bay. During winter the market also sells coon and muskrat meat. Notice the sign!

One newcomer worked the bay for five years before he was finally accepted by the other watermen. And, that was only after a waterman's boat had broken down on the bay and the "newcomer" had towed the man's boat to Port Mahon.

That deed seemed to have broken the ice and thereafter he was accepted. Delaware City, Smyrna Landing, Leipsic, Port Mahon, Little Creek, Bowers, Lewes and Mispillon are major docks for watermen from Delaware. Many of these watermen answer to names such as, Donnie, Jimmy, Freddy, Ronnie. Sammy, or Tommy.

When observed over a long period of time it is impossible not to have a certain amount of admiration for this group of men who still attempt to earn a living from the Bay. Especially when considering the decline in the number of crabs, fish, eels, oysters, and the low price paid for muskrat pelts because of a lack of interest in furs. And not least, ever changing rules and regulations governing their occupation.

When economic conditions are bad on the bay, many watermen seek regular employment, and just as soon as conditions get better, they return to the bay. It is almost as if working the bay is genetic. Toward spring many men who have worked the bay in the past start thinking of crabbing again. It becomes a fever. Many envision riches to be gleaned from the bay. One man once caught 12,000 peeler crabs in one day netting over three thousand dollars. Many people have hoped to do as well. That seldom happens. But Crabbers can still dream.

Working the bay requires a special type of person. One who wants to be his own boss; One who is very independently minded, and is not easily frightened by the dangerous conditions often found on the bay. In sum a waterman is a special breed set aside from others.

There have been men who have worked the bay for their entire lives, and some very successful. The older watermen are dying and with them dies a way of life, a time that will never be repeated.

CHAPTER 2

The Net Fisherman

In February or early March, depending on weather conditions, whether it is an early or late spring, the waterman stakes out his net for Trout, Shad, and Rock Fish. The water is still cold and the demand for fish is usually good at this time of the year.

Fishing with a net in early spring is a cold and dangerous occupation. Usually small flat boats are used. Most often they are made from wood and have no floatation devices built in like a recreation boat would have. These boats are usually powered with two motors. Most prefer 25 HP or 40 HP motors. Johnson Outboard motors seem to be the motor preferred because of their reputation of dependability.

"Herb" Mills displays the Striped Bass he hooked in the bay.

The Net Fisherman

In all kinds of weather the net fisherman tends his nets. He usually starts as near day light as possible because normally there is less wind at that time of the day. The fish can be easier removed from the nets when the water is calm.

One good aspect of net fishing during early spring is that there are less recreational fishermen on the water because the fish seldom take bait until the water warms to about 55 degrees. It is good that the Bay isn't swarming with sports fishermen during the net fishing season. Otherwise, many nets would be destroyed by recreational boats snarling their propellers in the nets. This usually destroys a large section of a net and creates bad will between sports fishermen and commercial net fishermen. Many sports fishermen resent the net fishermen and would have net fishing made illegal if they had their way. There is something to be said about each point of view. After all, watermen have the right to follow their trade as they and their fathers have for generations.

The net fishermen usually returns from the bay cold, exhausted, and sometimes a bit sea sick, and always filthy from the blood and gore from the fish that were entrapped in the nets. At the dock, there will often be a buyer to purchase their catch. Many times the price will be lower than the waterman expected or is willing to take. If he refuses to sell to the buyer, there is always the option of taking the fish to Rock Hall, Maryland, about forty miles away, and hopefully receive a better price from fish buyers operating there.

Many watermen attempt to create their own market in the local area. Usually there are people who desire fish for their freezers each year, and many local restaurants prefer to buy the local catch because it is fresh. In early spring Shad is in demand for its roe. The only stipulation from buyers is that a dependable supply of fish be available.

Marketing the fish is a constant battle. It would be interesting to see if the buyer's attitude would change if they had to take the fish from the nets. Braving the elements found on an unpredictable body of water such as the Delaware Bay takes guts.

Considering all of the danger, filth, and cold, the watermen still prefer earning their living on the bay to any other occupation. There is something to be said for being independent. The watermen are about the most independent group of people anywhere. Being one's own boss is many people's dream.

One such person was Billy who had followed in his father's footsteps and worked the water from an early age. He operated out of the Mispillion River, near Milford, Delaware, and tended a 400 yard gill net in the bay north of the Mispillion River outlet each spring.

His catch had been good for the first week of the season. He had a good market, which is very important to a waterman. Billy had contracted with several restaurants and supermarkets within the Milford area. The price was good and everything pointed to a good year. Maybe he could afford a new pick-up truck if the catch continued to be good.

It took him about thirty minutes to motor down river to the bay. Two 40 HP Johnson motors propelled his twenty-two foot wooden boat into the bay and to the empty gallon plastic milk jugs marking the start and termination of his net.

The day before he had taken over 900 lbs. of Trout, Shad and Stripe Bass from his net. He hoped that today's catch would be just as good or even better. The expectation of another good catch bolstered his spirit. Perhaps this year, he thought, he would make some money. Several seasons in the past had produced a meager return. A waterman has to be optimistic to work the water. It is hard work, but the rewards could be great.

The water was calm, the sky somewhat overcast, with a light fog hanging over the water. There was a chill in the air. He started pulling his net over the boat and taking the fish from the net. The catch was rather disappointing, only about 100 lbs.

Billy knew that he wouldn't have a good catch everyday, but his catch was much smaller than he had anticipated. After a cup of coffee from his thermos, he cleaned his boat, and started back for Milford. Hopefully, tomorrow's catch would be better. After all, it is difficult to predict how many fish would become ensnared in a net. People working the bay were accustomed to disappointing catches.

The following day was overcast, with a light wind blowing from the west as he motored down the Mispillion toward the bay. As he passed a launching ramp he observed a small, but new appearing boat being loaded onto a trailer. The individual loading the boat didn't even wave or acknowledge his passing. The man was a complete stranger which wasn't unusual.

The man at the dock was loading two coolers in the back of his pick-up as Billy passed. Billy thought that it was nice that someone else was catching fish. After a time he came to his net. The water was a bit rough, but he was accustomed to boisterous weather during the ten years that he had worked the bay. Today the catch was even more diminutive than the day before.

Could someone be stealing his fish before he arrived each day? Billy didn't want to believe the obvious, but someone must be pilfering fish from his net. He had heard stories from other watermen about losing fish and crabs to thieves, but he had never experienced people stealing from his net.

Billy grew angry and discouraged as he motored up the Mispillion River to Milford. To consider someone stealing from his net made him furious. He didn't steal from others and he wouldn't knowingly tolerate anyone stealing from him. He had worked hard to earn the money for his boat, motors, nets and other equipment and to have someone steal from him was just too much to accept.

He took the time to contact and apologized to each of his fish customers for the shortage of fish, and told them that he hoped his catch would get better soon. They agreed that it would be nice to keep buying fresh fish from him. However, they required a steady supply to meet the demands of their customers. If he was unable to supply their needs they would have to buy from someone else.

Billy decided to arrive at his net before daylight and wait nearby to determine if someone was really stealing his fish. After a routine trip down the river to the bay, he approached his net, a fog started drifting in, and soon the fog was thick and he could see only about five boat lengths through the fog. The water was dead calm.

He anchored his boat near the center of his net and sat quietly for over an hour. He sipped steaming hot coffee to ward off the early morning chill and patiently waited to see if anyone would approach his net and attempt stealing fish from his net. The early morning fog screened his proximity.

Finally, since no one had shown up, he decided to pull anchor and remove fish from his nets. He could see from the movement of the net in the calm, foggy morning, that he had a sizable catch. Just as he reached for the anchor rope, he heard the sound of a motor. He sat quietly for a time and soon a small white boat with a new 50 HP Evenrude motor appeared through the fog at just above idle speed.

The individual in the approaching boat cut the motor and coasted into the net. The man started pulling Billy's gill net over and across his boat and removing the trapped fish. He didn't see Billy until he was about four boat lengths away. He looked startled when he observed Billy sitting in his boat so near.

Billy angrily yelled, "What are you doing stealing my fish?" the person yelled back that Billy should mind his own business.

Billy answered, "It is my business. That is my net and my fish that you're taking."

The thief yelled back, "So what! What are

you going to do about it?" All the while he kept removing fish from the net.

This disregard for his property and the man's arrogance was too much for Billy. He reached to the bottom of his boat and picked up the 30-06 caliber rifle that he used for deer hunting in Maine each year, and pointed it at the other person. He was nervous and this was a new experience for him. He had never pointed a gun at a fellow human being before.

The thief saw the rifle and started cursing Billy. Calling him all kinds of names and telling him that he would take the rifle from him and stuff it up his rear end.

The boldness of the thief infuriated Billy, and that was the "straw that broke the camel's back" as far as he was concerned. Billy raised the rifle and fired one shot into the other fellow's engine, shattering the housing. Instead of retreating, the man picked up a paddle and started paddling toward Billy. He was cursing and threatening.

The man's violent behavior frightened Billy, and he fired two more shots into the new white boat. The bullets made small holes when they went in through the side and tore large holes as they exited on the other side of the boat below the water line.

From the angle Billy was shooting, the bullets entered just above the water line and exited on the far side bottom. Billy could see water pouring into the boat as he started his motors and left the area.

He never reported the incident to the authorities and the next day when he checked his net there were over eight hundred pounds of fish, and for the remainder of the season his catch was good and slowly ebbed as the weather grew warmer. That was normal.

Billy never again encountered the individual who he had caught stealing from his net. Near the close of the fishing season he happened to meet another fisherman whom he knew. They tied their boats together and shared hot coffee.

The other waterman related how he had found a very cold man floating on a gas tank near Billy's fish net several weeks before. It was a foggy morning and he had almost run over the man. The man was from Maryland, and claimed that he had been fishing when his boat had struck something which punctured its bottom, causing it to sink in a very short time. The boat and motor were both new and had cost him $4,000.00.

The man had failed to bring a life preserver with him and the only thing saving him from drowning was a half filled gas can. He had further stated that the Delaware Bay was too dangerous a body of water for fishing and that he would never fish there again.

The survivor of the boat sinking was a cold and scared individual. Billy could hardly restrain himself from laughing. It served the thief right. Maybe in the future he would think before stealing from anyone else.

CHAPTER 3

The Anchorage Area

Sunny days of May had finally arrived with reports of fish beginning to bite in the anchorage area of Delaware Bay. This area is a location where ships wait to lightened or to receive a pilot to guide the ship up the bay to Wilmington or Philadelphia. The water is very deep in this area. Many large fish such as Weakfish, Flounder, and Blues are in abundance during early spring. Jim invited Ray, who was a friend, and four men who worked with him for a fishing trip. All the men welcomed the opportunity to fish on the bay so early in the season.

Early on a Saturday morning, the 21 foot Mark Twain fishing boat was loaded with fishing gear, bait, and a supply of food to last the entire day. The plan was to motor from Little Creek,

Delaware where the boat was docked, and down the bay to the ship anchorage area and fish for the day.

That particular day was overcast with butter milk skies hanging low on the horizon. A wind was blowing toward the southeast against an incoming tide. This condition developed waves reaching four feet at times. It was a rough day, yet everyone was enthusiastic to fish. Reports of record catches from the anchorage area caused the men to toss caution aside and brave the rough water for an opportunity to catch some large fish themselves. They were dedicated fishermen.

Jim calculated that they had a sufficient gas in the event the weather continued to be tempestuous. Everyone agreed that even if the waves were rough, they still wanted to fish the anchorage area—some twenty-five miles down the bay.

Everyone had been in good spirits as the boat glided down Little River and out into the rough bay. Two of the men were already bragging about who would catch the largest fish. Soon the waves were running four to five feet, and Jim had to fight lofty waves and a fierce wind the entire trip down the bay. Several times the thought of returning to the dock entered his mind. He knew that everyone would be disappointed if he did abort the trip.

Several of the men became sick from the

constant motion of the boat smashing against large waves. However, the men agreed to continue the trip because the results would made the effort worthwhile. Even Ray had become quieter than normal. Jim suspected that he was also suffering from sea sickness. Several of the passengers were becoming quiet and turning pale.

Soon ships were sighted anchored in the deep water of the anchorage area. Jim neared the anchored ships, stopped the boat and threw the anchor out in about thirty foot of water, next to a drop-off into deeper water. The boat starting rolling so badly that everyone had to remain seated to fish. To stand up in the boat meant being pitched overboard.

Jim suddenly was hit with sea sickness. While he was piloting and steering the boat he was so occupied with fighting the waves that he didn't experience sickness. Once he had stopped the boat, the rolling motion of the boat drained his last resistance. He reclined on a canvas on the deck of the boat. After sipping a soda and closing his eyes for a few minutes, he begin to feel better and was able to sit up, bait his hook and cast it into the turbulent water.

After they had fished for a while, Jim turned on the CB radio and heard an announcement that "the small craft warning had been lifted." Perhaps they should have checked for a small craft warning before motoring through that stormy weather. Unknown to them, they had motored to the anchorage area in blessed ignorance of the weather conditions. After that trip Jim always checked the weather before taking any trip on the bay. The radio always gave an early morning weather forecast. It had been foolish to leave the dock in such bad weather.

  The first fish was caught by Stan. He had fished many times on the bay. He was jerking his bait with quick manipulations in an effort to attract fish. Suddenly, his rod bent double and he had a difficult time holding on to it. Everyone removed their lines from the water because it was obvious that Stan had hooked a big fish and they didn't want their lines tangled with his. He must have fought the fish for twenty minutes.

  Finally, Stan battled the fish until it was motionless in the water near the boat. The fish was the largest Blue Fish that Jim had ever seen. First he attempted to net the Blue. The fish was so large that it wouldn't fit into the net. Many times he had netted fish that were over three foot with that net. Next he attempted to gaff it and every time the point of the gaff would touch the fish, it would start flopping in a frenzy and bend the rod badly. Finally, when Jim jerked the gaff against the fish's gills in an attempt to hook and drag it from the water, the line became slack and it flopped up above the steel leader and bit the fishing line through, and then vanished into the depths of the bay. That fish was over five feet long. Needless to say, everyone was disappointed at the loss of such a large fish.

The next fish caught was a flounder weighing over seven pounds and after that fabulous catch the trout started biting. Ray immediately caught a twelve pound fish, and none of the several weakfish hooked weighed less than eight and one half pounds. Most weighed over ten pounds. Some of the weakfish were so long that their tails had to be bent to fit them into the thirty-six inch cooler. It was a fisherman's paradise—a once in a lifetime fishing experience.

Stan decided to use the CB radio and talked to different people who were fishing on the bay. He started telling the different people about how good the fishing was in the anchorage area. Stan really enjoyed talking and couldn't help but brag a lot. Ray felt like stuffing a sock or something in his mouth to get him to shut up. The damage had been done and the area soon became very crowded.

Within ten minutes boats started approaching the anchorage area from every direction. Soon there were about one hundred boats surrounding their boat. The large number of boats entering that area seemed to stop the fish from biting. Perhaps the schools of fish moved on to another area because of all of the disturbance from boats moving into that area.

Once the fish quit biting, Jim cranked the motor and they cruised back to Little Creek. The water was reasonable calm most of the return run up the bay. No one got sea sick on the return trip. Everyone was in a jovial mood.

The fish coolers were so heavy that two people were required to remove each from the boat and onto the pickup. That fishing trip was the best that most on the boat had ever experienced. It was a fishing trip worth telling about time after time. And they did!

CHAPTER 4

The Hook Incident

The enticing news that fish were biting on the Delaware Bay spread like a rumor. It seemed that every sports fisherman in the area decided to attempt catching their share of weakfish, blues, croaker and flounder.

Dave, his son, Ray, and Jim launched Dave's 18 foot boat at the Port Mahon ramp and motored down the river to the Bay and then followed the buoys northeast toward the state oyster beds where the fish were reported to be in large schools. Several fish weighing 12 lbs. had been reported hooked from the oyster beds.

The sun was rising with little or no wind. The conditions were ideal for fishing. The men had enough soda and sandwiches to last the day. They intended to fish the entire day, or as long as the

The Hook Incident

fish would bite. Peelers and squid were in ample quantity for bait. Overall, the day promised to be a good one. They could hardly wait to wet their lines.

They soon reached the state oyster beds where several boats were anchored. Dave selected a spot and threw out the anchor and everyone prepared their rods and reels. Jim was cutting bait for everyone. Dave's son was the first to bait his hook and cast his line. (It seems humorous that people would motor a mile out in the bay, anchor and then try to toss their line as far as possible).

The son whipped his new serf rod over his shoulder for a forward cast, and hooked Ray through the top of his shoulder. The large hook was buried completely in his bare shoulder.

Everyone felt badly for Ray having that large hook imbedded in his shoulder, but at the same time they wanted to fish. After all, the fish hadn't been this plentiful in many years.

Reluctantly, in a disappointed sounding voice, Dave stated that they had better pull anchor and return to Port Mahon so that Ray could be taken to the hospital emergency room and have the hook removed. Ray wanted to fish too and he sensed the disappointment in his friends.

The boy was apologizing to Ray, Jim, and his father for ruining the fishing trip by being careless and hooking Ray. He looked and acted so remorseful that one would think he had murdered someone.

Jim made the mistake of asking Ray if the hook hurt. Sarcastically, Ray answered "only when I smile and I don't intend to smile for a while." Surprisingly, there was little blood flowing from the hook wound. The large hook was buried completely in his shoulder. Looking at the hook-imbedded shoulder almost made a person sick. Jim thought to himself, "I'm sure glad the hook is in Ray's shoulder and not mine." Of course he wouldn't have dared to verbalize such thoughts.

Ray looked around the boat. There was Dave looking somber, his son embarrassed, and Jim looking wishfully at people in other boats pulling in fish. Ray wanted badly to fish, too.

Finally, after a moment of silence, a silence so deep that dropping a pin would be loud, Ray asked Jim if he would attempt to remove the hook from his shoulder, and if he could, they would stay and fish.

Everyone looked relieved at not having to immediately leave the fishing area. Jim was more than willing to attempt removing the hook. After all, it wasn't his own shoulder that had the large hook firmly embedded. Meanwhile, he baited and tossed his hook overboard so that he might entice a fish to bite while he was busy with Ray. Why miss an opportunity to catch a fish?

Jim located a knife and pliers in his fishing box and removed some of the rust and bits of rotten squid attached to the blade. Dave and his son immediately started fishing. After all, only one person was needed to remove the hook. There was no sense wasting time watching and most likely being in the way when they could be fishing.

Jim first attempted to remove the hook by pushing in through the skin so that he could cut off the barb and then pull the hook out. That was the way he had read that hooks with barbs were removed. The entire operation appeared an easy task from what he had read about the procedure.

Exerting all his strength failed to push the hook through the skin so the barb could be removed. Somewhat frustrated, he next attached the pliers to the hook and still was unable to push the hook through the skin. Ray was sporting a deep tan which had toughened his skin. The only solution was to cut the skin so that the barb could be pushed through.

Ray's normally deeply tanned face was pale by the time Jim yanked and pushed on the buried hook. Finally, Jim cut through the tough skin with the not-too-clean pocket knife, pushed the hook through, cut the barb off with the pliers, and then pulled the hook back and out of Ray's shoulder. Jim was rather proud of the manner he had successfully operated on Ray's shoulder. If they had taken him to the emergency room, what could they have done differently?

Jim, seeing the paleness of Ray's face, made the mistake of asking if the ordeal hurt. Ray only looked at Jim like he was an dimwit and said nothing. His silence spoke louder than words. Once the hook was removed only a few drops of blood dripped from the wound. A band aid was applied and Ray was ready to fish.

The fishing trip was a success after all. They caught a large number of fish (60), enjoyed their sandwiches and sodas, and later in the afternoon returned to the dock. At the dock, it was discovered that neither Dave nor his son had ever cleaned a fish. Good old Ray cleaned the fish for them—all 60. He did an excellent job too.

Ray's shoulder healed without infection and he was soon ready to go fishing again. He was always careful after that incident to suspiciously watch others when they cast their bait into the water. One hook imbedded in a shoulder was sufficient to last a lifetime.

Chapter 5

Sharks

Delaware Bay is a breeding ground for several species of sharks. Schools of sharks make their appearance once the water warms and remain until the waters starts to cool. Most are harmless and small. However, sometimes there are exceptions to the size of sharks found in the bay. One crabber motoring out of the Mahon River into the bay in his 30 foot boat slammed into what is believed to have been a large shark. The impact shook the entire boat and alarmed the boat's occupants. A large shark like fish skipped across the water after the impact before submerging into the cloudy water. The occupants of the boat estimated the creature to be about twenty foot long.

Many years ago, three people crabbing by the bridge in Little Creek, Delaware were treated to a sight that they didn't care to see too often. One of the men noticed a ripple in the water coming toward where they were crabbing. The tide was high and the water calm.

To their horror, the ripple was recognized as being caused by the fin of a large shark. They leaped back from the edge of the river bank and watched in fascination as a large shark swam under the bridge. The men rushed to the other side of the bridge and watched the shark turn and swim back down stream. When the shark turned they could see its teeth from a partially opened mouth. The shark completed its turn and once again passed under the bridge and finally cruised out of sight down the Little River. The shark appeared to have a length in excess of ten feet.

Only thirty minutes before the appearance of the shark, three young boys were splashing around in the water in an attempt to cool off because it was a hot and humid day. Perhaps they were more fortunate than they would ever know.

The Shark Fishermen

Two airmen from Dover Air Force Base, Delaware had heard about the many sharks to be found in Delaware Bay and decided to see how many they could catch on an outing into the Bay.

They thought it would be fun and maybe exciting to hook a big shark.

For fishing equipment, they had procured beer kegs for floats, large hooks, and 1/16 inch steel cable. Bait was hunks of rotten beef. They thought that bait would be appetizing to sharks.

Before launching their boat into the bay at the Bower's Beach ramp, one of the men drove to a chicken processing plant near Milford, Delaware and collected two five gallon buckets of chicken entrails. The chicken entrails would be dumped into the water near the floating beer kegs. Hopefully the extra bait would help attract sharks. It was a hot day so they brought along two cases of cold beer. The men thought that perhaps the beer would make their day more relaxing and keep them cool.

The day was excessively hot and overcast with hardly if any wind. The bay was calm as a table top. This condition seldom occurred. The boat was 14 foot long and powered by a 10 HP Johnson motor. The boat was much too small for the bay on most days, but because of the calm water at that time, it was suitable.

The men baited the large hooks and tossed six beer keg floats into the water about seventy-five feet apart. Next the buckets of chicken entrails were dumped in the middle of the floating beer kegs. The tide was high and slack, so they sat in the boat enjoying cold beer while awaiting the action to start.

After about ten minutes one of the kegs started slowing moving. They chased it down and found a seven foot Thrasher shark hooked through the side of its mouth. One of the men immediately shot the shark several times with a .22 caliber rifle brought along for the occasion. They gaff and pulled the still struggling shark into the small boat. Immediately several steaks were cut from the shark and placed in the large cooler. They tossed the remains of the shark back into the water.

The hook was rebaited and tossed back into the water. While they were drinking beer and waiting for another shark to be hooked, a ripple could be seem approaching the boat. At first the ripple only attracted mild attention, then to their chagrin, a large fin was seen near the boat. Soon the water was disturbed by the large shark devouring the remains of the shark they had just thrown over board. They could hear the sound of the flesh being torn. The sound was chilling.

To their horror and dismay the shark was longer than their 14 foot aluminum boat. The large shark swam around their boat several times and approached near enough to have struck it over the head with their paddle. Of course, the scared men didn't dare hit the shark, or even to shoot it with the rifle. It was just too big! Imagine injuring the shark and making it angry. To be dumped into the water with such a large shark was something that they didn't care to experience. They held their breaths until the shark was further from the boat and was just started to circle back in their direction. The operator of the boat thought, "Lord, help this old motor to start on the first pull of the starter rope." It did!

The encounter with the large shark had completely terrified the men. The boat's operator accelerated the motor and headed toward shore as fast as the small boat could move. The shark headed in their direction and vanished into the depth of the bay. Each occupant of the boat imagined the shark chasing them. As far as their were concerned the beer kegs could float around the Delaware Bay for ever. There was no way they would attempt to retrieve their shark rigs. After the encounter with the large shark their enthusiasm for shark fishing dissipated. Land had never looked so good to them.

A Desperate Situation

Jim, who worked on the water part time, set his gill net south of the Little River outlet near Pickering Beach, Delaware. He experienced good catches of Weakfish for two weeks. When the weather turned unseasonably warm, the water started warming and there was a danger of fish caught in a net spoiling before being removed. He always checked the gills of fish caught in his nets to determine if they were freshly caught—white gills indicated a fish had been dead for considerable time, pink showed that the fish was fairly fresh, and red revealed the fish were freshly caught.

On a clear, warm morning Jim motored to where the net was staked out with the intent of removing any fish ensnared and to take it up for the season. He pulled the net over the bow of the open boat and started removing fish enmeshed there. The catch was good as he proceeded along the net. It was filled with large Weakfish, some Manhaden and several small Sand shark.

The tide was ebbing and because of a light wind there were swells that would lift the boat gently up and down. Suddenly he noticed that something was eating the trout caught in the net. When the boat rose and fell with the 2-3 foot swells, he noticed that there would be large trout in the net and then when the swells dropped the boat lower, and it would again rise out of the water, the trout would be chopped to pieces. Often where there was a whole fish in the net when it dropped, then there would be only a head remaining in the net when it again rose.

Peering in to the cloudy water, Jim observed sharks four and five foot in length hungrily devouring the fish caught in the net. He didn't mind losing a few fish, but the sharks were eating almost all the remaining trout. It appeared that an entire school of sharks had arrived and were in a feeding frenzy. He had never experienced sharks feeding on entrapped fish like he was seeing. It was frightening to observe the sharks tearing the fish apart. That scene could just as easily be a man being eaten. Some of the sharks were following the net up when it rose with the swells and would fall back into the water.

Occasionally, when the net would come out of the water, a shark would be trapped. Jim would stab the shark in the head with an ice pick before removing it from the net. He then gutted, washed and packed the sharks into the cooler. He had heard that shark steaks were tasty. They proved to be delicious!

Jim saved all the trout that he was able before taking up the net. The net was one hundred yards long and it took some time to remove the fish from the net, clean the fish heads and other trash from the mesh. Finally the entire net was rolled up on the boat with all that remained to be done to finish the job was untie the net from the pole where it was attached.

Hanna

Oops, Lost My Boat!

The net fisherman had just pulled his gill net into the boat and loosened the net from the pole when the tide pulled the boat from beneath him. The net had been filled with fish and the sharks were in a feeding frenzy. He was barely able to pull the heavy boat back underneath him. He felt that the sharks would have been happy eating him along with the fish.

He untied the knots securing the net to the pole. He was holding on to the pole with his right hand and using his left hand to pull the last of the net into the boat. The tide had started to run strongly by that time and unaware to him, the boat was being pulled out from under him. He found himself in a serious predicament. He was left clutching the pole with both hands and his legs were stretched to their limit and only his feet were holding the boat.

He had almost panicked when the boat had slipped out from under him. He was over a quarter of a mile off Pickering Beach, and the water was full of hungry sharks feasting on the remains of fish caught in the net. The boat weighed over a ton. It took all of his strength to tense his body and pull the boat back under his body.

He was convinced that the sharks would have eaten him just as easily as they were devouring the trout. At one point only the tips of his toes were holding him on the boat rail. Once the boat was again pulled under him, he gave a sigh of relief and sat down in the boat to regain his composure. He remembered in great detail the sharks feeding in the water only three feet under him.

Some people even dare to water ski on the bay. One day Jim observed an Aqua-Sportsman boat cruising back and forth off Pickering Beach near where he had the incident with the sharks feasting on the fish caught in his net. Two very attractive young ladies were water skiing and would occasionally fall and splash around in the water. He was sure they weren't aware of the huge concentration of sharks in the water all around them. There are many watermen who would never consider swimming in the Delaware Bay. Sometimes ignorance is bliss.

CHAPTER 6

Crabbing

One season several years ago crabs were scarce on the bay with daily catches hardly sufficient to pay for the gas or diesel fuel expended operating the boat to check all the crab pots. Few crabs were being caught on the bay. Most of the crabbers pulled their pots in disgust after several disappointing days working the bay, and gave up crabbing for the year as a lost cause. The lack of crabs was very discouraging to men who had approached the new crab season with great anticipations for a profitable year. For the rest of the summer many hired on as carpenters and did lawn work to earn a living. Some were more fortunate because they were employed and working on night shifts, and then crabbed during the day. It was a tough schedule for them, but the security of a job when crabs was scarce was very beneficial.

Hanna

Ronnie Virdin's Boat

Crabbing

The Lone Crabber
Several crabbers work alone on the bay. This crabber is experienced at dealing with crisis situations while working alone. It can still be a dangerous job.

"Hard times" is an appropriate name when crabs are scarce on the bay. David Dill, crewman checks the boat.

Fish Used For Crab Bait

Treasure From Delaware Bay

"Peeler" crabs are highly valued by sports fishermen for bait, and by restaurants for soft shell crabs. — A peeler is a crab in the process of molting (shedding its shell). Before the new shell hardens it is a delicacy in great demand in many seafood restaurants.

Crabbing

The "Hard Times" with a cargo of 12,000 peeler crabs. Skipper Wayne Mills had something to smile about. It was a good day on the bay.

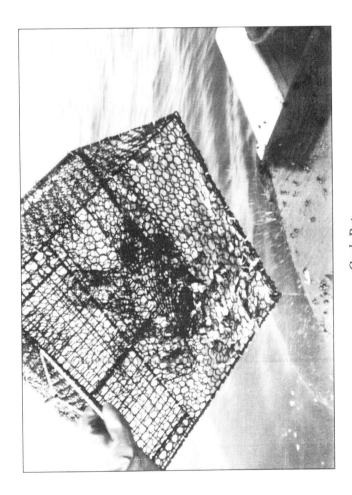

Crab Pot
(*A wire basket designed to catch crabs*)

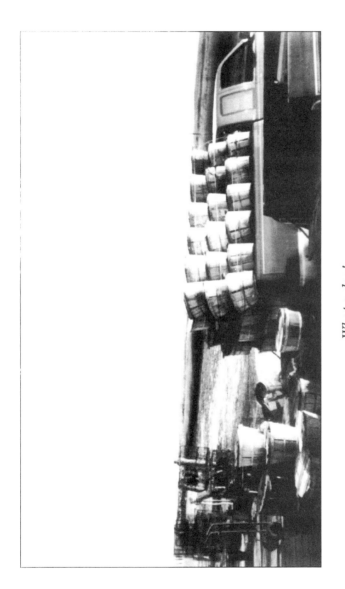

What a day!
A problem that all crabbers would like to experience...not sufficient space on the truck to haul the day's catch.

Young Crewman Emptying Crab Pot
Many young men work as crewman on crabbing boats. Most aspire to own their own boats. There are some third generation crabbers still working bay. Crabbing and fishing is the only occupation in which they care to work. Some people will tell you that working the bay gets in a person's blood.

Crabbing

Cleaning the boat after a day of crabbing

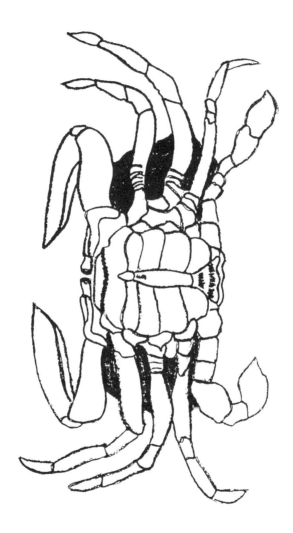

Male Blue Crab "Jimmy"

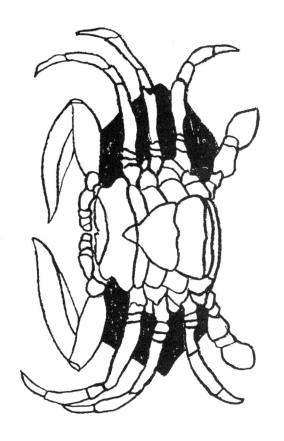

Female Blue Crab "Sook"

One unemployed crabber was driving through the small village of Lebanon, Delaware and where the road paralleled the St. Jones River, he observed numerous people "chicken necking" on the shore. Those people were catching crabs, some large size, with a chicken neck tied to a string and dropped into the water. Crabs would start eating the chicken neck and the bait was slowly pulled toward the surface, and the hand-held net could be dipped into the water and catch the crab. Several people had baskets and five gallon pails filled with crabs.

Seeing all the crabs being taken from the St. Jones River inspired the crabber to rush home and call his crabbing partner. Early the next morning the crabber and his partner were motoring down the bay from Port Mahon to the mouth of the St. Jones River. The 30 foot crab boat was loaded with crab pots. The channel into the St. Jones River is narrow and tricky, but the crabber skillfully piloted his boat into the channel and up the river.

The crab pots were baited and dropped into the river all the way up stream to near the sleepy village of Lebanon, Delaware. They decided not to venture further up steam from fear of detection. Commercial crabbing in streams was unlawful, but the crabbers considered that they were encountering troublesome economic times, and they were willing to take the chance of evading the Marine Police.

For several days they were able to harvest a large number of crabs and were able to pay off some of their bills. However, all good things never last. Their luck ran out one day when a Marine Police boat suddenly appeared around a bend in the river and confronted them. Someone had observed them setting crab pots in the river and had reported them to the Marine Police. After discussing the bad economic conditions caused by the shortage of crabs on the bay, they were told to immediately removed all their crab pots from the St.Jones River. Also, if they would agree to never commercially crab again in the river, no charges would be pressed. Obviously, the crabbers accepted that proposal from the Marine Policeman. They felt fortunate not receiving a large fine for violating the law.

Facing a large fine and a loss of their crabbing license was a situation that they didn't care to face. It took them all day to pull in all the crab pots they had placed in the river. They had experienced record catches of large crabs in the St. Jones River. Having to dump the captured crabs back into the water went against the grain. Since they had no choice, they released all the crabs found when their crab traps when retrieved.

Non-commercial crabbing is limited to two crab pots per person. A Teacher who taught at a local school would drive to school with a canoe attached to his pickup rack. After school he would drive to Lebanon, launch his canoe and check the two crab pots he had set out down stream from Lebanon. Once he took a friend along who wanted to see how crabs were captured and perhaps help tend the traps after school each day. His friend expected to receive some free crabs for his effort.

The two crab pots yielded almost a basket of large crabs. The teacher decided to relocate his crab pots. He paddled the canoe to a bend in the river and asked his friend to grab a willow limb to steady the canoe while he baited and threw the pot back into the water. He was wearing coveralls and gloves. Standing up in a canoe isn't too good an idea at best, but he did any way.

He tossed the heavy crab pot toward the middle of the stream and a wire on the pot caught his glove, and since he was off balance standing up in the canoe, it pulled him overboard and head first into the water. The water was only about eight foot deep at that point. He held his breath until reaching the bottom of the stream where he was able to loosen himself and resurface.

When the soaked man surfaced, his friend was doing his best to keep from falling into the water too. The canoe was about half filled with water, and crabs were floating in the water that had rushed into the bottom of the canoe when it was tilted. The crabs had escaped from the basket used to contain them. It was a comical scene watching the friend attempting to keep from falling into the water and at the same time evade the angry crabs. He was wet up to his knees and several crabs had grabbed his pant's legs.

The teacher waded ashore and pulled the canoe into shallow water and bailed most of the water from the canoe. He used a net and recaptured most of the crabs and placed a lid on the basket. He was covered with mud, and of course soaking wet.

The men paddled the canoe back to where the truck was parked and unloaded their crabs and placed the canoe back on the rack. It was a hot day and the stream bank was lined with people "Chicken Necking" with a string and hand net. Most hadn't caught very many crabs at that time. A small boy came over and was looking at the basket which was over two thirds filled with large crabs. He asked " Mister, how did you get all them crabs?"

The man who was soaking wet told the small boy that his partner used him for bait. When the crabs came after him, his partner would scoop the crabs up with a net. The boy believed that story and started running down the edge of the river telling everyone about the men and their unusually manner in catching crabs. Several came over and looked at the large crabs, and the evidence backing up what the boy had told them was standing before them. The teacher was still dripping water as he and his partner entered the truck and drove away. The other people who were crabbing were talking and pointing in their direction.

Thereafter the teacher had to crab along because his partner decided that crabbing from a canoe was too risky. One of the crabs had pinched the calf of his leg and that had hurt.

Toward the close of the crabbing season the catches on the bay increased, but not to the extent that anyone earned much profit. Crabbing has always been a chancy occupation. An outsider probable wouldn't understand the love of working on the water and the independence enjoyed from working for one's self.

During the same period of scarcity of crabs on the bay, a commercial crabber placed a dozen pots in the sloughs and runs adjacent to the Leipsic River a few miles below the small village of Leipsic, Delaware.

It is about eight miles from Leipsic to the bay. There are several places where someone could crab unnoticed. One stream runs off the Leipsic River and connects with the Simmons and the Mahon Rivers. That area is a maze of sloughs and dead end inlets. Most of the old timers know their way through that area. Setting crab pots in the river was illegal and the man was well aware of that fact. He was desperate to attempt catching crabs in the river and sloughs because few were being caught on the bay. He successfully crabbed in the river for several days.

He would check his pots before daylight using a spotlight. He knew the channels like he knew the back of his hand. He had crabbed all his life. He was very happy with the amount of crabs he was catching. Crabs for selling for a very high price because of their scarcity. Catching only a few baskets of the big number one jimmy (called so by crabbers) crabs was the equivalent of catching a large number of baskets of smaller crabs the size being caught on the bay.

One foggy morning at 4 AM, he cruised slowly into a slough off the Leipsic River to check his crab pots. He was using a spot light to locate the floats marking each pot. The floats were plain cork without any identification to reveal the ownership of the crab pots. After all, surely the Marine Police wouldn't get up that early so he would be safe from detection. He thought he would never be caught.

He was shining the light toward where he thought a crab trap was located when the beam of the light outlined a boat moored in a lead off the slough. Then he was illuminated and startled by flood lights. It was the Marine Police who were waiting for his approach. The man was in trouble because aboard his boat were seven crab pots that he was relocating, and about a basket of freshly captured crabs still dripping water. He attempted to talk his way out of the situation, but the Marine Officers refused to be swayed by his pleads and then finally threats.

The crabber was arrested on the spot by the Marine Police and his crab pots were taken for evident. All seven of the new crab pots were taken for evident along with the freshly captured crabs.

The crabber was furious about being caught in the act of illegal crabbing in a river. To show his contempt for the Marine Police, once he was at the dock, the stomped the seven new crab pots flat, thereby rendering them useless for crabbing. The Marine Police made no comment regarding his temper outburst.

At the trial, the illegal crabber was fined and as he tromped out of the court, the judge stopped him and inform him he could have his crab pots back, since the court never kept crab pots taken as evidence in a case. This pronouncement really upset the man. He had no idea that his pots would be returned to him, otherwise he would have never damaged them beyond repair like he did. He receive considerable teasing from his friends about having stomped his crab traps flat, then having the pots returned to him.

CHAPTER 7

Woodland Beach

On a misty day in June, a crabber who lived near the Bay departed Port Mahon and after reaching the open bay set a course north for Woodland Beach. The water was somewhat choppy with a wind blowing from the northwest. Otherwise, it was a good day. The mind of the boat operator was not on crabbing. He was thinking of the big profit he was to make from the deal he was about to consummate. He had borrowed ten thousand dollars from the bank, and had mortgaged his boat and car as security for the loan. He was to meet a schooner off Woodland Beach and transact a deal of a lifetime. Crabbing hadn't been too good, but this transaction would turn his ten thousand dollars into near one hundred thousand. That was almost as well as a politician's wife recently did on the stock market.

His heart skipped a beat as he noticed flashing lights in the distance as he neared Woodland Beach. Also, he observed several other boats fast approaching the schooner. There were signs of activity on the shore. He knew that something had gone wrong. He recognized a Coast Guard vessel and a Marine Police boat approaching the schooner.

The man turned his 30 foot boat 180 degrees and pushed the throttle to maximum power and headed back for Port Mahon. He realized that the authorities were aware of the transactions taking place at Woodland Beach and were moving in for the kill. He knew that soon they would observe his boat and be in hot pursuit. Surely, the authorities must know the identity of all persons involved in the transaction. He was scare someone would squeal on him.

All of his plans for a quick profit had gone awry, now he risked forfeiting everything. His boat, truck, and home could be seized. He kept looking back over his shoulder for a Marine Police boat to begin the chase. His big Chevrolet motor was purring like a kitten and moving at thirty miles per hour. Normally he was afraid to open the boat to full throttle because prolong operating at that power setting could ruin the motor. Now he had nothing to lose. At least he wouldn't give the authorities the satisfaction of impounding his boat. Such is the case when a person is apprehended in a drug arrest. From the start the deal seemed too good and too easy to be true. The person he had dealt with from the start had told him that every enterprising young man all along the coast was doing what he was planning. Dealing must be okay since many people he knew were involved and seemed to profit from their efforts. After all, crabbing hadn't been too good lately.

    He turned into the Mahon river and selected a section of the river where he could run the boat upon the bank. It was high tide, so he barely slowed down and went sliding through the grass and debris and came to a jarring stop. That was no way to treat a boat, but he didn't care because he was going to lose it anyway. He jumped out of the boat, picked up the five gallon can of gas that he always carried for emergencies and emptied the contents over his boat. He was determined that the authorities would never get his boat. He stepped back from the gasoline soaked boat, lighted a rag and tossed it into the boat. The boat lit up like a torch, and he ran for his pickup and sped for home.

    He rushed into his house, locked the doors, and threw himself into a chair. He was shaking from head to foot. What should he do now? He knew that any minute he would hear a car or cars pull into his driveway, and there would be a rapping on the door and he would be arrested. At least he possessed enough cash to post bail.

The man suffered a night of agony, with the TV and radio on to alert him to any new developments on the raid. He heard nothing until the seven AM local news. Then, he heard an announcement about a big drug bust at Woodland Beach. The news indicated that all participants had been arrested. The schooner was taken in tow by the coast guard, the captain and two man crew had been arrested, and twelve cars, RVs and pickups had been confiscated by the authorities.

In all, about twenty people had been arrested and charged with possession and dealing in illegal drugs. There was no mention of pending arrests or of him. Perhaps they didn't know that he had been in on the deal to purchase illegal drugs? Had he burned his boat for nothing?

From the start the authorities had been aware of the schooner and its activities. The boat had been under surveillance since it depart Florida and sailed up the inland water way. All the stops and deals the crew had made had been carefully documented.

A day before the drug bust twelve vehicles of varied description arrived in Dover, Delaware and registered in local motels. Each vehicle was either towing or carried a small boat on roof racks. Their purpose in town was to travel to the nearby small coastal village of Woodland Beach, and buy drugs from a schooner scheduled to arrive the following day.

The next day the men drove to Woodland Beach, and one at a time were allowed to row out to the anchored schooner and buy drugs. The schooner's captain was careful to allow only one person at a time to board his vessel.

The State Police were well aware of the transaction taken place and once all the vehicles had driven to Woodland Beach, set up a road block at the intersection of state road 9 and the Woodland Beach road. There was no other way out of Woodland beach by road. The drug dealers were trapped.

The people purchasing drugs departed the beach immediately after making their purchase and were stopped at the road block, drugs confiscated, read their rights, and held under guard until all the dealers had been nabbed. They were then driven to jail under escort of the State Police. The police performed brilliantly in handling that drug bust.

The man burnt his boat for naught. The police never knew that he was a part of the "Big Drug" deal.

CHAPTER 8

Stories from the Bay

Jim worked the Bay for five years and had diverse experiences, some dangerous and some humorous. He operated a 21' boat, powered by a seventy horse power Johnson Motor. Many times he felt that his boat was too small and felt imperiled by the storms and resulting high waves often encountered on Delaware Bay. Overall, working the bay on a daily basis was an unique experience.

Often people would travel on the bay with him for the experience. Whenever possible, and in most cases, Jim enjoyed taking someone with him while he pulled his crab pots, removed fish from nets or fished with a rod and reel. The bay can be a lonely place when one works there alone day after day. He experienced and knew of many unusually incidents that occurred during the years he worked the bay.

Following are some of the incidents he experienced or was aware of occurring on Delaware Bay.

Anchor Problems

On an overcast day, with a light wind blowing, causing two foot waves and swells, four men from Pennsylvania were fishing from a 16' boat. They had never been in the bay before and were excited by the expectation of catching varied and large fish. They were motivated by stories told to them by several friends who had many time successfully fished the bay. They were almost in awe of the vastness of the bay.

They were really excited about their first fishing trip on such a large expansion of water as Delaware Bay. Because they had never fished on a large body of water before, they didn't understand the danger lurking on the bay. One thing they did wrong almost immediately was anchoring their boat incorrectly. In a river or small pond it would make little difference how a boat was anchored, but it did on the bay!

The men made the mistake of tying the anchor rope to the stern of the boat instead of the prow which is the proper position for the anchor rope. When there are waves and wind such a mistake can cause many problems.

The wind increased and the water became more choppy as the day progressed. Because of the anchor rope being tied to the stern of the boat, waves started washing over the rear of the boat. Finally a larger wave hit the boat and filled the boat completely.

The boat was constructed with Coast Guard approved floatation. Still, the boat settled so low in the water that the motor was flooded and everything in the boat that would float, floated from the boat.

The men, almost in panic, were able to slip into their life vests before the boat settled in the water. When the boat was filled with water, it became unstable. The men clung to the sides of the boat for over two hours until another boat came by and rescued them. One man died from exposure. Later, a larger boat from Bowers Beach towed the water filled boat to the boat ramp.

Two weeks later, Jim was traveling from Port Mahon to Bower's Beach. Off Kitts Hummock Beach, about a half mile out, he sighted a small boat occupied by three men who were fishing.

That boat was anchored from the stern and water was coming aboard and the men were bailing as fast as they could. Jim eased his boat to within talking distance, cut off his motor and asked them if they were having a problem.

One of the boaters answered, "no, nothing we can't handle."

Jim told them they would soon have trouble if they didn't move the anchor rope to the bow. He related the incident of two weeks previously. The men thanked Jim for his concern and he proceeded on to Bower's Beach.

He was sitting in a restaurant on the dock having breakfast when he observed the men whom he had met and talked to on the bay, motor into Bowers and tie up at the dock. Jim finished breakfast and walked toward his boat. He encountered the men who had just docked. He asked them why they came in so soon. (They had previously told him they were to fish all day) "Have you caught all the fish you want?" he asked them.

The men informed Jim that he had scared them badly with his story about the incident of the boat swamping two weeks previously. They, too, were from Pennsylvania and had never fished on a big body of water like the bay.

One of the men said that after Jim had stopped by and told them their anchor was wrongly attached, they started viewing the bay differently and became scared. In other words, they laughingly told him, "You ruined our fishing trip by relating how the other boat had almost sunk." They told him that the bay had become very intimidating after he had left.

Jim told them he was sorry about scaring them, but it was important to anchor a boat properly. The men thought their response regarding the entire affair was humorous and offered Jim a cup of coffee.

The New Boat

Jim and the men from Pennsylvania were enjoying their coffee, when he noticed a new boat in the process of being launched. It had never been in the water before. A man and his wife were taking their first trip on the bay with their own boat. They had a proud look on their faces. The 17' boat was a fine looking craft. The women had even made frilly covers for the boat seats. Obliviously, the couple were proud of their new acquisition.

The channel into Bowers Beach is very narrow and a boat exiting or entering Bowers must stay within the channel or else run aground on a hard sand bar. Several people have learned the hard way about the sand bars bordering the channel.

The just-launched boat's operator, almost immediately, accelerated to top speed and started down the clearly marked channel toward the bay. The boat operator definitely wasn't observing the "no wake" speed. The boat must have been going 30 miles per hour leaving a large wake behind. Boats were rocking from the huge wake left by the passing boat.

Jim watched in disbelief as the boat abruptly turned north and immediately ran aground. Spray and sand flew into the air and the boat came to a jarring stop, catapulting the occupants from their seats and into the water. Fortunately the couple was not harmed from the dunking in the water. Mostly there were only shook up from the unexpected and jarring stop.

Other boaters had observed the incident and immediately assisted the couple to free their boat. Soon several people were wading in water little more than knee deep helping to drag the boat from the sand bar. The man and women only suffered a few scrapes and bruises—nothing serious. They would probably have sore bodies the next day.

Once the boat was pulled into deeper water, it was turned around, the motor restarted and slowly made its way back to the launching ramp. The return to the dock was vastly different than the departure had been. Both husband and wife looked embarrassed because of the incident.

No one likes to be thought of as an amateur, but they definitely were. It had been humiliating to have run their boat aground, especially with all the onlookers. And then, just think, people had to come to their assistance. However, they must have been thankful for not suffering serious injuries when thrown from the boat into the water. A few scratches was a cheap price to pay for an incident that could have been worse.

Jim examined the boat once it was out of the water and on the trailer. The bottom of the hull looked like it had been sand-blasted down to bare fiberglass and the prop was missing one inch on each blade.

Just before the couple entered their truck and drove away, Jim heard the women say to her husband, "just as soon we get back to Dover, we're going to sell this stupid boat." The woman made that statement just like it was the "stupid boat's" fault they had run aground. Jim had to laugh at that comment.

Was the Bay That Bad?

One year a man from Reading, Pennsylvania purchased a new boat and with several friends, traveled to Mispillon near Milford, Delaware and launched the boat. That boat ramp was a favorite for many sports fishermen because launching a boat from that ramp shortened the run to the anchorage area where fishing was normally excellent.

The first part of the day went well until late in the afternoon when a storm blew in from the northwest against an incoming tide, therefore creating enormous waves. Delaware Bay can, from a dead calm, become rough in a matter of minutes. All that is needed is the right combination of wind and tide. Such were the conditions that day!

The boats caught in the rough weather were bouncing from wave to wave and many people became very sea sick. The men in the boat from Pennsylvania, having never experienced anything like that storm, were especially affected. They thought they would never arrive back to land. They were a happy group when the channel markers came into sight.

The boat owner tied up at the Mispillon Marina and after their equipment was removed and loaded into their station wagon, he turned to a group of people standing on the dock and tossed the keys to his boat toward them and said "any one of you who wants the boat can have it, I will never fish Delaware Bay again."

He got in his vehicle and drove away. The boat was turned over to the Marine Police for disposal. The Marine Police, through the boat's registration, contacted the man and he admitted that he was done with boating and they could do what every they wanted with the boat. When he had finally came ashore he was so thankful to be safe that he lost all interest in fishing or boating again on the bay. His action was unusual at best.

Heavy Cargo

Jim made an agreement with a bait shop operator in Little Creek to sell his crab catch on consignment each day. The bait shop would sell the crabs and pay Jim the next day. This arrangement worked to the satisfaction of both Jim and the bait shop owner. That venture supported the bait shop all summer.

One day Jim checked his crab pots and returned to the bait shop with the day's catch. He was greeted by a man named Bert who often hung out at the shop and would enjoy a cup of coffee with him. Bert asked Jim if he would grant him a favor.

Since Jim knew the man, it wasn't like a stranger approaching him with a request. The man wanted to know if Jim would take his father-in-law fishing on the bay. His father-in-law had always dreamed of a fishing trip on the bay, but the opportunity had never arisen. Hopefully, Jim would take them to the bay fishing.

Jim told the man that he would be glad to take him on a fishing trip. He instructed Bert to tell his father-in-law to be at his Little Creek dock at seven the following morning and they would fish for a while.

When Jim arrived at the docks the next morning, the man and his father-in-law were waiting him. The father-in-law created a problem. Jim's friend had failed to tell him anything about his father-in-law. He was the biggest man that Jim had ever seen. He was about five feet four inches tall and as round as several barrels. Jim discovered that the man weighed 658 lbs.

Jim kept his promise to take the man fishing. The tide was three feet below the docks and incoming. Jim, and Bert assisted the heavy man to sit on the dock. The boat was tied to the dock in several places to stabilize it so the big man could slide along the dock, drop his legs over the side, and then ease down into the boat. There was a seat in front of the center console. The man seated himself on that seat and didn't move the entire trip.

The bay was rough and later Jim discovered that the big man had never fished from a boat before. Not only had he never fished from a boat, but he had never been on a boat. He was soon sea sick and attempting to keep from throwing up. The man's face was a ashen grey and he said that he wished he could die. Jim gave him a soda in an effort to calm his stomach. The drink helped by soothing the man's stomach to some extent. His sea sickness never completely dissipated and he suffered the entire trip.

They fished for about an hour, caught a few fish, and then return to the dock at the man's insistence. Unloading the man was a problem. A heavy man travels down better than up. The tide was even with the dock and Jim again tied the boat in several places to the dock.

With assistance from Jim and Bert, the man was able to struggle out of the boat and on to the dock. He was very appreciative of Jim giving him a trip to the bay.

He said that he had been scared half to death because of the rough water. He didn't know how to swim and had been worried about the boat capsizing and being able to locate a life preserver that would fit his tremendous size and weight. It was all he could do to keep everything down from the boat pitching in the waves. That had been his first time on the bay and definitely his last.

The Fisherman

Often, when stopping by the Little Creek bait shop, Jim would be introduced to different people who had stopped by for crabs, bait, or other items. At that time many people stopped by the shop and chatted over a cup of coffee. One day when Jim entered the bait shop he was almost overcome with laughing. What was so funny? Four older men were sitting at a table drinking coffee without shirts with their big bellies sticking out. What a disgusting sight to people who didn't know them.

On many occasions people would ask to be taken fishing. One of those asking one day was a man whom Jim had never seen before. The man politely inquired about fishing in the bay and asked to accompany him fishing the next morning. He stated that he was new in the area and enjoyed fishing. Jim told him he would be happy to have him along for the trip. Sometimes it got lonely on the bay.

Jim, George, an acquaintance, and the newly introduced man motored down Little River to a calm bay and a beautiful day. Hardly any wind was blowing and the tide was coming in. It was a good fishing day. Birds were flying in huge flocks when disrupted by the approaching boat. It was a splendid sight.

At the oyster beds off Kitts Hummock, Delaware they used peeler crabs for bait and were soon hooking weakfish. Fishing was a dream! Every time a hook hit the water a fish would hit. The man who had accompanied Jim asked why they didn't use artificial bait and lures.

Jim just laughed, and told the man that peeler crabs were the best bait to use to catch large numbers of fish. After all, they had over fifty fish running 1-3 pounds. The man asked Jim if it was alright for him to use a lure. Jim had no objection. However, he thought the man foolish to use a lure when the fish were being caught with hooks baited with peeler crabs. It was hard to criticize their bait when considering the large number of fish they had already hooked.

The man caught ten fish in about twenty minutes and none weighed less that six pounds. Some of them weighed ten pounds. Jim couldn't believe what he was seeing. The man used a peculiar jerking motion when reeling in his lure.

Jim switched to a Bucktail lure and tried to duplicate the other fisherman. He caught nothing. At the end of the fishing trip, the cooler was full, with all the large fish having been caught by the other fisherman.

At the dock, the fish were divided. Jim and George got the fish they had caught. The man thanked Jim for the fishing trip, loaded his large fish and gear into his car and drove off.

Jim never learned the man's last name, but he did know that he had been fishing with a master fisherman.

Chapter 9

The New Boat

The man purchased a new boat at a local marina much to his wife's disapproval. She had never been in a boat in her life. Her husband had ventured out on the bay on a head boat once and had fished the St. Jones river a number of times from a canoe with a friend. That was the sum of his experience. He had decided that there was a lot of fun to be found on the Delaware Bay in a nineteen foot boat with his family and friends.

The man worked at General Foods in Dover. Earned good money and had good credit. There was no problem financing the new boat and he proudly towed the new boat home and parked it on his lawn. It appeared large sitting on the new galvanized trailer. The first thing he did was wax the boat like a person would a new car. It not only shined with an high gloss—it glared.

Owning a new boat was fine, But what about the equipment needed to operate on the Delaware Bay? Three thousand dollars later, with new fishing gear, floatation devices for his family and friends, a new depth/fish finder and a CB radio, and not forgetting the Coleman cooler to keep fresh the fish they were sure to catch. Now he was ready for the first trip as a family on their new boat into the beautiful Delaware Bay.

He decided to launch the boat at Port Mahon near Little Creek, Delaware for the family's first fishing trip. After all, "the family that boated together stayed together." He liked that quote. He had adapted it from "the family that prays together, stays together." He felt sure that no one would object to his misquoting that old saying.

There would be no such thing as him making his wife a "fisherman's widow" by being away fishing all the time. His entire family would share the excitement of motoring on the Delaware Bay in the hot summer. He could already imagine the cool breeze blowing in his face as he cruised on the bay.

He had already canceled the family's reservation for a trip to Disney World. Why travel all the way to Florida when Delaware Bay was only a seven mile drive from home? His family would spend weekends the entire summer on Delaware

Bay. Forget staying home on Saturdays, forget going to church on Sundays. (Most people in his church were away most of the summer anyway. Besides, all the Pastor preached during that period were reruns).

For the entire summer he and his family could enjoy time together on the Bay. Besides, he would be able to stock his freezer with many species of delicious fish. Hadn't he read that eating fish was healthy and lowered cholesterol. From the sun, relaxation, and fishing the summer promised to be an enjoyable season.

On a sunny Saturday in June the man awaken his family at six in the morning. Somehow his family mistakenly thought that Saturday was a time for sleeping in. He had a very difficult task awakening the entire family. No one seem to want to get up for a good breakfast and a trip to the Bay. He thought it terrible to sleep when there was such an exciting time awaiting them on the Bay.

By the time everyone was up and eating their cereal for breakfast, he was raring to go. The entire family wasn't speaking to him by the time everything was loaded into the car for the trip to the launching ramp.

Both children were sound asleep before the car and trailer were out of the drive. His wife, with a sleepy voice, asked him if he was sure that they should go boating and fishing? After all, the family's only day for sleeping in was Saturday and she felt that she needed that one day to recuperate. Besides, she had to get up early the rest of the week to prepare breakfast for him and the children.

Her question resulted in him lecturing her regarding the hard task he had of toiling each day for a company that didn't really appreciate his efforts. After all, he needed something to do so he could relax and fish away the frustration generated by his difficult job. His wife heard him out and thought to herself, "This husband of mine should assume the role of housewife and mother and see what generated frustration is really like." Wisely she kept her thoughts to herself.

He told her that she just didn't understand the situation and should be more supportive of his plans for the family. "Remember, our children are growing older and we need something to do as a family to keep them a part of the family." She agreed that the family should do things together, but why boating? He just stared at her like she was ignorant and said nothing.

No doubt it had been bothering him that several children in the neighborhood never did anything with their parents and they seemed to always be in trouble. He didn't want it to be that way with his family. To him the boat was the answer to keeping his family together.

Deep inside he felt somewhat guilty about spending all that money on the boat. He wanted to justify his expenditures in his own mind. His wife had wanted a swimming pool for several years and he had always told her that the family couldn't afford the cost. Now he had spent enough on the boat to have installed two swimming pools. Somehow the boat seemed more important than a swimming pool. If only she would be understanding! Of course, women were like that. Sometimes they just didn't understand. A man just had to do his thing. After all men are different than women.

The drive to Port Mahon took longer than anticipated. When he had turned off the main road onto the Mahon road, he felt a drag from the trailer and it started swaying. Investigation revealed a flat tire. That was no problem because he had purchased a spare for the trailer.

His wife and children enjoyed sleeping while he changed the tire. By the time he had completed that task, he was wet with perspiration and covered with insect bites. The Green-Headed Fly bite was the worse. They sure were persistent and by the time he had completed the tire change there must have been twenty of those pesky insects attached to various parts of his body. Maybe he should have worn long pants instead of shorts.

He had never launched a boat at a boat ramp before. He had observed others launching boats and it didn't appear difficult. When he arrived at Port Mahon there was a large line of cars and pickups with boats and trailers behind. He wondered why they were parked and hadn't launched their boat into the river. He drove past the long line and saw an empty ramp and turned and started backing down the ramp.

Suddenly, almost everyone in the dozen or so cars and trucks started tooting their horns and some even making obscene gestures from open car and truck windows. "My, such a rude bunch!" he thought. He noticed a man in uniform—he was a marine policeman—who walked over to where he was attempting to back down the ramp and told him that he had to wait his turn at the end of the line.

"All of those fellows lined up are waiting their turn to launch their boats. You have to wait your turn," the marine policeman told him in a kindly, sort of amused tone of voice. This embarrassed the man and he drove back down the Mahon road to where he could turn around and get in line. His face was red from embarrassment as he passed the other men waiting in line. He received some hard looks and if he would have noticed, people were shaking their heads in amusement.

Forty-five minutes later the line had moved until it was his turn to launch his boat. He carefully backed the boat trailer into the water. He wondered how far he should back into the water. Finally, there was resistances like there were blocks preventing the trailer from entering the water further. He accelerated the engine and the trailer backed over the blocks and further into the water.

To his horror the trailer tongue came loose from the hitch and the boat and trailer started moving further back into the water. He jumped out of his car and quickly tossed a rope over the trailer tongue and attached it to the bumper hitch. With a squealing of tires and revving the engine, he was able to pull the trailer and boat back up the ramp and past the obstruction the he had backed over.

The Marine Policeman came over and told him that the obstruction was in the water to prevent trailers from backing too far into the water. He gave the man help in reattaching the boat trailer to the hitch.

After a few minutes the boat was tied to the dock, the car and trailer parked in the lot and very thing loaded aboard the boat. At last they were ready to motor down the river to the Delaware Bay.

The man felt a sense of satisfaction after finally launching his boat. After all, He reasoned, everyone makes mistakes until they can learn the ropes.

His family was by this time acting apprehensive about leaving the dock. The man thought that they would regain confidence in him after they were aboard the boat for a while. He only wished that they didn't appear so uninterested and almost scared.

The 150 HP Johnson Motor started with a purr. It was pumping water which showed that the cooling system was unobstructed. He liked the sound of the motor. The only thing that bothered him was that his youngest daughter suddenly blurted out, "Daddy, I want to go home," punctuated with tears. Her mother hugged her like the world was coming to an end or some other terrible disaster was about to strike. She was making the best of a very bad situation like all mothers are supposed to do.

He said, "Brace yourselves, here we go." He slowly pushed the throttle back to the reverse position. There was considerable disturbance in the water behind the boat, but the boat didn't move over a foot. Then he noticed that he had failed to loosen the two ropes holding the boat to the dock. Somewhat embarrassed, he positioned the throttle to neutral.

"John, now that I have tested the motor,

please loosen the two ropes holding us to the docks," he instructed his son.

After the ropes were removed, the boat slowly backed out into the river. The man accelerated the motor which set everyone back into their seats and the boat flew down the river leaving a huge wake behind. The boat must have been moving at forty miles per hour. "Just feel that power," he thought.

They flew past several boats—that for some reason were creeping down the river. They waved at every boat they passed and were disappointed at how rude the other boaters and the people whose boats were tied up reacted to their waving.

People were shouting at him something that he couldn't understand because of the noise from the motor. The gestures that the other boaters gave with their index fingers was easier to understand. The entire family—the family had come alive when they had raced down the river at full throttle with the wind blowing in their faces—was shocked at the rudeness of the other boaters.

Looking back they observed the Marine Policeman waving at them. They waved back. He was sure a friendly man. They didn't see him waving at any of the other boaters. It was good to know that at least he wasn't rude like the other boaters. Probably the other boats' owners were from out of state. He had heard talk about how rude many of the out-of-state boaters had proven to be.

As the boat moved toward the open bay, the man made a sharp left turn and the boat came almost to a complete stop and the engine popped out of the water and started making a strange noise. All around the boat was mud. They had gone aground.

He was going to write to the Marine Police complaining about them not marking the channels properly. However, further out in the bay he did see what appeared to be barrels floating in a long line several hundred feet apart. Floating barrels would really be a hazard for boaters, he thought.

After finally freeing the boat from the mud, the man spotted several boats anchored some distance out in the bay. He knew enough about fishing to realized they had found a "hot" spot and he was going to anchored near the other boats and catch his share of fish.

The other boats were about a mile off shore and it took only a matter of minutes to reach the area where about ten boats were anchored and people could be seen fishing.

The man decided he would look the site over before anchoring and fishing. He was in an hurry so he circled the anchored boats at a fast speed. After all, there wasn't any sense being poky when he had a fast boat. By the time he cut his motor and glided into the center of the other fishing boats, the water was churning and people were having to grab the rails on their boats to prevent being pitched in the bay.

He received many hostile stares as he tossed out the anchor. He yelled at the nearest boat, "Catching anything?" In reply the other fisherman only shrugged his shoulders.

Soon husband and wife had dropped their lines baited with squid into the water. Their two children didn't want to touch the squid. He figured that since fishing was new to them, he would allow them to observe how he fished and once he caught something they would become interested.

After an hour of fishing all they had caught were five oyster crackers. The first one he removed from the hook latched onto his finger and before he could sling it off and back into the water, his finger felt like it was caught in a vise. He then under stood why that fish was referred to as an "oyster cracker." If he was naming it, he would call it a 'finger cracker".

"I'm sick! I'm dizzy and sick at my stomach," both children declared at about the same time. To emphasize their point, both rushed to the side of the boat and regurgitated everything they had eaten.

While the mother was consoling the sick children, she, too started to become sick from looking down at the water from a gentle swaying boat. Soon she was regurgitating too.

The woman's unattended rod suddenly bent double and the line ran out with a steady clicking noise. At the same time, the man's rod also bent and the line played out. His wife had lost interest in fishing and he suddenly had two poles to attend. Since the rod holder secured his wife's rod, he decided to reel in his fish (it seemed from the drag on the line that it was a big one) and then attend his wife's line.

The man reeled in a struggling Thrasher shark. It was six feet long. He wondered if it would bite. Because of his uncertainty about the shark he was very careful in playing it close to the boat. Finally, he was able to gaff and heave the struggling shark into the boat. The shark was thrashing about and ended up against the legs of his wife who was bending over the side of the boat. She let out a scream that could be heard over the entire area. She grabbed the two children and retreated to the far end of the boat.

Apparently, that wasn't far enough, because she yelled at her husband to throw the shark back overboard. There was no way that he would even consider tossing the catch of a lifetime (for him) over board. He attempted soothing her by emphasizing the point that the shark was harmless and would make good steaks.

After repeatedly stabbing the shark to insure that it was dead, he covered it with a sheet of plastic. Meanwhile, his wife's line had run out to its fullest extent and was entangled with two lines from the nearest boat.

The other fishermen were standing in their small boat attempting to untangle their lines from the woman's. A large ray had been caught on the woman's line and was swimming in circles with the other two lines entangled with the woman's.

Finally, the two men cut their lines, started their motor and departed the area. The man waved at them, but they appeared rude and ignored his friendly goodbye wave. "Some people are grouches," he thought as they motored past. When he was able to work the ray close to his boat he was awed by its size. There was no way his wife would remain on the boat with a huge ray struggling all over the boat. Reluctantly he cut the line leading to the gyrating ray.

"We want to go home this minute," his wife told him in an angry tone. He had seldom seen his wife so angry. He knew that if he didn't obey her and start for home, he would suffer the silence and retorts his wife was good at for weeks.

The motor started with a purr and he accelerated, fully expressing his disappointment at having to leave the fishing grounds before he was ready. He left a huge wake as he guided the boat through the fishing area near where other boats were anchored. He could see people grasping boat rails and sides of boats to maintain their balance as he flew through their midst. He drove the boat angrily like he did the car when he was irritated.

His wife and children were holding on for dear life and all were in tears. After a short time his conscience started bothering him so much that he slowed the boat, and finally stopped and turned off the motor.

He decided that he had better make peace with his wife. He moved to the prow and bent over his family and started telling them how sorry he was that they had gotten sea sick. He insisted they drink Seven-Up and eat some crackers he had brought along in the event anyone would become sick. That seem to help matters somewhat. But, everyone still wanted to go home as fast as the boat would take them.

The man decided that before returning to the dock, the family should enjoy a nice boat ride. Everyone was feeling better once they were again underway. They were in one-half mile of the Mahon river when the motor sputtered once or twice and stopped completely.

"Oh no!" he thought to himself as he checked the gas tank. It was empty! "You dummy, didn't you have enough sense to bring along sufficient gas for this stupid boat? What are we going to do?" his wife screamed through tears.

"No sweat, someone will come by and tow us in or lend us gas," he retorted.

He tossed out the anchor and almost immediately his wife and children, and he too, somewhat, were sea sick. What a miserable feeling. The entire family was so sick that they were afraid of dying, and then, became afraid they wouldn't die and be relieved of their misery.

Soon other boats from the fishing grounds passed. He attempted flagging them down. He was completely ignored as the other boats sped by leaving large wakes. His boat was rocking from the waves generated by the passing boats. The more the boat rocked, the sicker the entire family became.

After enduring sea sickness for about four hours, and after there was nothing left to regurgitate, they wished they were dead. Finally, the man told his wife that he was going to pull anchor and drift toward the mouth of the Mahon River.

The water was somewhat rough because of a freshening wind. The boat was slowly being blown toward shore. He planned to toss the anchor onto the shore and once the boat touched land he would jump ashore and walk across the island to where he would find help.

He tossed the anchor toward shore when the boat neared, jumped, landing in mud about waist deep. Somehow he swam through the mud and pushed the anchor deep into solid land. He was covered with a black stinking mud.

His wife and children were being tossed about somewhat badly. They appeared in no immediate danger, so he started walking across the marsh toward the Mahon docks.

It took the man a good half hour to reach a point across the river from the boat ramp. He attempted to attract the attention of boaters. After a time someone spotted him and paddled over and asked if they could be of help.

Soon, carrying a two gallon can of gas loaned by a boater, he started the walk back across the marsh to where the boat was anchored. When he arrived, the boat was sideways to the waves and half filled with water. His wife and children had donned their life vests and were trembling in fear.

He had a difficult time reaching the boat with the gas can. Somehow he made it to the boat. He bailed the water from the boat and managed to pour about a gallon of the gas into the boat tank.

Soon he was underway and arrived at the docks in short order.

Once at the dock he was abandoned by his sick wife and children who immediately climbed into the car and closed their eyes. They were still pale and sick. All they could do was moan as they reclined on the car seats. He didn't feel much better.

The next day anyone driving through his neighborhood would see a large sign on his lawn. It read "BOAT, MOTOR, AND TRAILER FOR SALE CHEAP"

CHAPTER 10

A Just Reward

It was a beautiful day on the Delaware Bay. It was a Sunday and a day of rest for the crabber. At that time state law prohibited commercial crabbing on Sundays. Still, Ronnie was up early and using his small fishing boat, soon arrived at the point of land where Little River flowed into the bay. He stopped his boat behind the sand bar and sat back with the intention of spending the day if necessary watching his crab line. The colors identifying his crab pots were red-green-red, and almost every Sunday when he wasn't working on the bay someone was stealing from his crab pots.

The fact that someone was taking a few crabs from his pots didn't bother him too badly. The thing that really made him angry was that whoever was stealing from his pots was leaving the trap door open. Leaving the door open on a Sunday resulted in several, sometimes a dozen, pots without crabs when he checked his line on Monday. Any crabs attracted to the pots would enter and then after eating the bait, exit through the opened door. He was determined to discover who was stealing from his crab pots and put a stop to it.

He sat and drink coffee from his thermos and patiently waited for about three hours before he noticed a small white boat approaching his crab pots. Several times boats had motored past his crab line without stopping. This boat had slowed as it neared the crab floats.

Watching through his binoculars, he saw the occupants of the small craft stopping at his crab floats and pulling in pots. The people in the boat would quickly empty a pot and toss it back into the water without closing the trap door.

Stealing from crab pots wasn't anything new. Some crabbers not only lost crabs from their pots, but on occasions someone would take a large number of crab pots. Each pot cost more than twenty dollars when fully rigged with floats, zinc, rope and metal weights. Often the pots would be stolen and taken to another area of the bay with different identifying colors attached and reset. Attempting to relocate stolen pots is like looking for the proverbial needle in a hay stack.

A ex-crabber, Eugene (Shorty) Short was one of the first watermen in this area of the bay to use wire basket crab pots. He had an entire line of crab pots stolen. He immediately placed more crab pots in the same location, and hid in the reeds on Kelly Island armed with a 30.06 rifle for two days waiting for the thieves to attempt stealing the new pots. He planned to riddle the thieves' boat with rifle fire. He was that angry!

The marine police—I think they were called something else in those days—discovered what he was up to and promised to watch his pots and attempt to apprehend anyone caught stealing. They never caught anyone, but the stealing from "Shorty" stopped. Word must have gotten around that a person might just get shot for stealing some ones' pots. Stealing still goes on. The author lost a string of fifteen pots over night and never relocated them.

Ronnie became infuriated when he observed the people in the pleasure boat emptying his crab pots. He, like other crabbers, worked hard on the bay. Often he had to confront adverse climatic conditions and poor catches in an effort to earn a living. And, here he was observing someone systematically stealing his crabs. He possessed a quick temper and now he was mad. The waterman decided to teach the thieves a lesson they wouldn't soon forget.

The man started the boat's outboard motor and rapidly approached the boat holding the crab thieves. Nearing the boat he observed an older couple and a small dog as being the only occupants of the boat. He was normally very polite and respectful of older people, but this couple had gone too far. He had no respect for these two because of their stealing from him. If someone wanted crabs and didn't have money to buy them, he would gladly give them a mess of crabs to eat.

Ronnie docked his boat along side the drifting pleasure craft and grabbed an axe from his boat, jumped into the other boat and started chopping a hole in its bottom. He hadn't said a word to the couple in the boat. They had seen him approach, but to them he was just another boater passing. They quickly retreated as far as possible from the axe wielding apparently psychopathic man who had jumped into their boat. On a small boat one can only retreat so far. They were speechless and appeared half scared to death. Who wouldn't be under such circumstances? Water immediately begin to pour into the boat from the holes chopped in the floor, and Ronnie leaped back into his boat and accelerated back toward Little River.

The last view of the boat he had chopped a

hole in, it was settling in the water and the two were donning their life vests. The couple finally regained the courage to yell something at him. Maybe they were asking for help. He had ignored their appeals (he guessed it was an appeal for help, he couldn't and didn't want to hear what they were saying) and continued toward Little River and his dock.

He heard later about a couple whose boat had sunk in the Delaware Bay. The couple had remained in the water for over two hours and had drifted three miles with the tide before another boat had discovered and rescued the pair floating in their life vests. The dog had drowned.

The couple never attempted to explain to their rescuers the circumstances that led to their boat sinking. They told the rescuers that "something had happened to their boat and it had sunk." Perhaps they realized that being caught red-handed stealing from crab pots and the attack on their boat was a just reward for their unlawful act.

After that incident, Ronnie had fewer problems with people stealing from his pots. yet, some people still think it's okay to take a few crabs from a waterman's pots,—"after all the crabber won't miss a few crabs." He was sorry about the dog drowning. The poor animal was an innocent party.

CHAPTER 11

Overnight on the Bay

It was a sunny, but somewhat cool October day and the trout (Weakfish) were still in abundant supply in the bay. This would be one of the last opportunities to catch a good number of these evasive Weakfish.

Sammy's boat was old, but still serviceable. The only problem was that his motor was in bad condition and couldn't be depended upon to start when you wanted it to start or could it be depended on to run continuously when needed. So Sammy was able to borrow a new 40 HP Johnson motor from a man who had recently moved to the Little Creek area. The new man thought that loaning a local waterman something would help build a friendship.

This Waterman was a well known character in the Little Creek, Delaware area, and it wasn't difficult to borrow a motor from someone new to the area. Old timers in the Little Creek area knew Sammy, so they wouldn't have loaned him a boat or motor. He wasn't known for taking proper care of his equipment. However, he was a nice guy and almost everyone liked him. Sammy had served in World II and was wounded in Europe. He never talked about his war experiences and lived a modest life. Years ago he lived in an old house on Pickering Beach during the summer and in the winter, he moved about a mile inland into an old house in the woods. He led a hand to mouth existence and was often helped by the local people.

Sometimes when the man agreed to help on a crab boat, he would agree with all sincerity and with good intentions. One crabber hired him to work on his boat and when Sammy failed to show up, he drove to the house where Sammy was living at that time. He blew the truck's horn and the man failed to come out. The crabber became concerned that maybe the man was ill. He entered the house and found it to be empty. The bed looked like it had been recently slept in. Out of curiosity the crabber open a closet door to see if Sammy's coat was gone. To his amazement, Sammy was huddled in the closet attempting to hide. It was early (5 am) and very cool. Sammy had consumed a few beers the night before and just couldn't face working on the bay that day.

He would do such things as placing a two hundred yard net out in the bay and then seldom check it to remove the ensnared fish. Often, when he would finally check the net, it would be full of hundreds of rotten fish. The neglect of his nets created bad will toward Sammy from many fishermen, both commercial and sports fishermen. Lucky for him the Marine Police apparently weren't aware of his waste of fish. His intentions were good, but somehow he never got around to checking his net daily as he should.

Anyway, Sammy was able to borrow a new 40 HP Johnson outboard motor to use on his old leaky boat for a fishing trip, by himself, to his favorite fishing spot about two miles off shore in the oyster beds. If one knew the bay well, he could find many schools of fish. The oyster beds were usually a good place to fish. Sammy had worked the bay for so many years that he knew most of the good fishing spots. He knew the bay like one knows the back of one's hand.

As Sammy later related, everything went well for the first part of his fishing trip. He arrived to the oyster beds without any problem and the bay was smooth as a table. No one else was fishing that late in the season. He was used to being alone so that didn't bother him.

He immediately caught several good size trout and fished until he used all his bait. Later in the afternoon, He happened to glance to the Northwest and observed dark clouds forming. The wind started to blow and with the wind came large waves.

Often storms will follow the bay and Sammy was no stranger to bad weather and storms to be found on the Delaware Bay. He decided to start for home and pulled on his anchor rope and it broke just above the anchor.

Breaking the rope and losing the anchor didn't bother Sammy because he had borrowed the anchor, so it wasn't his loss. He had earned a reputation of never being overly concerned when he lost something he had borrowed. Yet, he would give a person the shirt off his back if he saw a need. He started the motor and headed back toward the entrance to Little River. When he was about a mile off shore the motor started missing and finally stopped completely. Try as he might, he was unable to restart the motor.

By this time the wind had become stronger and the temperature was dropping. The boat was too large for using the one aged and very rotten oar that he had brought along. The waves were increasing into threatening heights and the boat was bouncing and taking on water faster than Sammy could bail it out.

Sammy needed an anchor badly to keep the bow into the wind. Since he had already lost his anchor, he did the next best thing. He loosened the new Johnson motor and tied the anchor rope to it and dropped it overboard to serve as an anchor. It worked fine. The waves must have reached about six to eight feet and the water was very cold.

Just before darkness, two crabbers who kept their boats docked in Little River noticed that Sammy's boat was missing. The only person who knew that Sammy was out in the bay fishing was the person who had loaned him the motor.

The man didn't know what to do. His main concern was having Sammy return his motor and a mess of freshly caught fish he had been promised. The motor owner planned to store it for the winter. He mentioned to one of the local weathermen that Sammy had borrowed his motor and had not returned with it. The waterman remarked that Sammy was honest in that he would always return anything that he borrowed, even if it was misused.

The fact that Sammy hadn't returned from the bay created some concern. The temperature was dropping and the wind was still blowing hard out of the Northwest. He could have gone into

Woodland Beach, Port Mahon, or perhaps beached his boat at the Kitts Hummock settlement or Picketing Beach, that is if the water was calm enough.

The next morning the temperature had dropped into the low thirties and no one had heard from Sammy. The man with whom he lived drove to Little Creek and asked different people if they had seen Sammy. He was worried about Sammy failing to return home the night before.

Herman Moore, a well known, and highly respected waterman decided to start a search for Sammy. The weather was deteriorating rapidly and turning colder. To be trapped on the bay in a disabled boat was a serious matter.

Shortly after clearing the mouth of Little River, Herman sighted Sammy's boat in the distance. As he neared the boat he could see that it was swamped with only the bow sticking out of the water. He thought to himself that old Sammy had finally taken too many chances and drowned himself.

When Herman's boat came along side the swamped boat, he observed movement in the small bow recess used for storage, and Sammy waved and asked to be taken aboard. He was soaking wet and shivering from the cold. He had spent the entire night wedged in the small recess of the bow of the boat.

Sammy was wrapped in blankets and given a cup of hot coffee. His improvised anchor, the 40 HP Johnson, motor was retrieved and the boat towed back to Little Creek. The salt water had ruined the motor's electric wiring and ignition system. The newcomer was out one motor. He learned a valuable lesson regarding loaning equipment to people he didn't know too well.

The victim didn't receive even a cold from his overnight exposure on the Delaware Bay. Later, Herman Moore, in answering a comment about how fortunate Sammy was to have survived overnight in the cold water, remarked that "it had been so long since Sammy had taken a bath that the cold water couldn't penetrate through the dirt and tough skin."

He was one of the tough individuals who attempted to earn a living from the bay by means of crabbing, fishing in the summer and trapping muskrats during the winter. To survive in a waterman's occupation, one had to be tough. Sammy was such an individual.

CHAPTER 12

Trapping

Trapping muskrats has been an age old occupation for many watermen. The marshes of Delaware have produced huge quantities of muskrat pelts. During the depression era many people earned their living in the winter months trapping the plenteous muskrats found in the marshes. Some of the marshes were so productive that a person could almost walk across a marsh stepping on top of the muskrat houses.

After the last of the crabbing equipment has been stored for the winter preparation begins for the winter muskrat trapping season. The pelts of muskrats, raccoon, otter and fox becomes an important source of income during the winter.

Because of protests from animal rights groups the age old occupation of trapping isn't followed as it once was. Man made fibers have replaced the use of animal fur compared to that of the past. Because of protests and the use of new fibers, the price of muskrats has dropped drastically. There is little money to be made trapping a marsh under present conditions. Trapping is done mostly for the thrill of being in the outdoors and the exercise gained from walking and wading through the marshes. Also there is the satisfaction of being knowledgeable enough to place a trap where an animal will be in the future.

Delaware Bay is surrounded by streams and marshes abounding in wildlife. Today, trapping no longer attracts the large number of people that it once did. However many watermen still pursue this age old occupation. The flesh of raccoon and muskrat is still enjoyed by a large number of Delawareans.

Preparation for the trapping season usually starts in late November. People can be seen cutting 6 to 8 foot poles and checking traps for serviceability. Flags or streamers are tied to the poles so that the traps won't be lost forever in the marsh. The trapping season usually starts about mid-December and continues into early March. For a novice, trapping the marshes can be a dangerous occupation.

Trapping

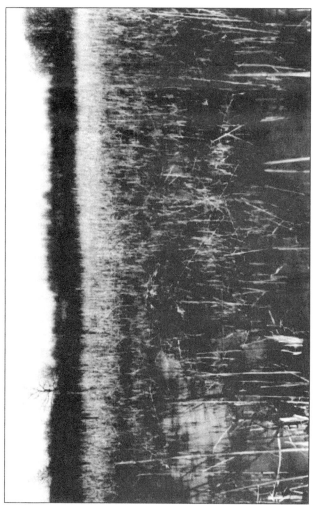

A Muskrat House in the Marsh

Muskrat trapping was once an important industry on the Delaware Bay marshes. While this occupation has declined in recent years, many people still trap as a sport and for economic reasons. The flesh of muskrat is eaten by many Delawareans.

Trapping can be a family affair
Bill and his sons, Jeff and Kevin with a day's catch of raccoon.

Trapping

Delaware Trappers Skinning A Raccoon

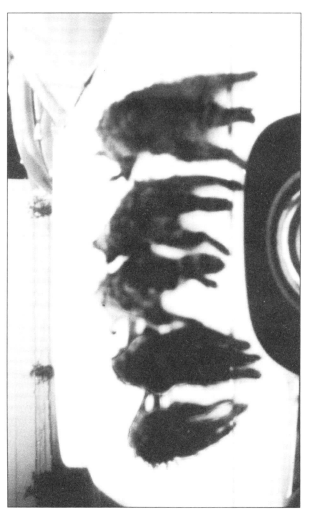

A Days Catch Of Raccoon From The Marsh

Raccoon Trapping is still pursued by many Delaware outdoorsmen. In many homes raccoon meat is served during the winter months. Nothing is wasted from the raccoon. The pelt and the meat are sold. Many Delaware fish markets sell the flesh of fresh caught raccoon and muskrat.

Trapping

Trapper Joe
Joe was a part-time trapper who waded the marshes after work each day. Most often he would check his traps after dark by flashlight.

One trapper related some of his trapping experiences. He trapped alone and because of taking a full time job for the winter, he operated his trap line after work which would necessitate walking the marsh after dark. Often the tide would only be out later in the evening and he would wait until then to tend his traps. It is a must for a trapper to tend his traps daily.

Walking the marsh at night can be an exciting experience, especially when the tide starts coming in and the ditch that normally can be waded at low tide is fast filling with the incoming tide. Such an event occurred one cold January evening. Ice was floating in with the tide and the trapper knew that he had to make an effort to cross the forty foot wide ditch immediately before the incoming tide completely filled the ditch and stranded him in the marsh until the next outgoing tide. He wasn't prepared to spend a cold and wretched night in the marsh.

The trapper was warmly dressed and wearing chest waders. He started to carefully wade across the ditch. Soon the water reached within one inch of the top of the waders. For a time the depth remained the same. He was feeling confident that he could manage to successfully wade across the ditch. When about twenty feet from the far side of the ditch he suddenly stepped into soft mud and immediately sank under the surface.

First, there was an inclination to panic. Then the trapper rapidly realized that his only chance to survive was to keep his head. The waders quickly filled with water and his clothing was soaked. He knew he couldn't reach the surface and remain above the water because of the weight of the water filled waders, so he swam and pulled himself on the bottom and climbed up the far bank of the ditch. He crawled out of the water like a muskrat coming out of the water. He was covered with mud and thoroughly soaked. The temperature was in the twenties. He lost his cap, but was thankful to be able to climb up the stream bank and out of the water. He had held his breath until it felt like his lungs would burst.

The trapper started to remove the waders and then decided that keeping them on would preserve some body heat. He still had to walk about a mile to where his pickup was parked. He slowly sloshed through the marsh until he reached the pickup. He immediately started the motor and turned the heater to full. While he waited for the motor to heat up, he kept walking around the truck to keep warm. By the time the interior of the truck was warmed, he was shivering over his entire body. He experienced difficulty removing the wet outer clothing.

The woolen long underwear and shirt apparently had helped maintain some body heat. Never had he enjoyed such a welcomed heat as he experienced in the cab of the pickup truck. Once he had warmed up, he suffered no further repercussions from his exposure to his late night swim in the freezing waters of the tidal ditch. Needless to say, he lost the few muskrats he had been carrying when he had sank under the water. Somehow the loss of a few muskrats didn't matter compared to what could have happened.

When a trapper walks his trap line he never knows what problems he may experience. It is very important that a trapper be tough and fast thinking. Those two factors can save a person's life.

CHAPTER 13

The Trapped Trapper

Trapping in the marshes of the Delaware Bay can become very hazardous and sometimes deadly because of the deep mud and quicksand. Often a trapper will wade tidal ditches at low tide because muskrat holes are located in the bottom of the ditches. However, most trapping occurs on the marsh in the muskrat leads. Muskrat leads are trails worn in the mud from these animals traveling to and from their houses. Some of the ditches are filled with soft and often deep mud. This condition can create a situation whereby the trapper becomes trapped.

Such an incident occurred on the St. Jones River below Dover, Delaware. A trapper was checking his traps at 4 AM during low tide. He had already caught and removed several muskrats from his traps and was feeling good about his efforts in trapping a new area. The beam of his flashlight revealed several muskrat leads (trails) in the muddy stream bed. He set several connibear killer traps in those leads. This trap is a very humane means of killing muskrats. A muskrat swims through the jaws of this trap and is killed instantly. He was able to lean over the ditch and using a long pole with the trap attached, set the traps in place. Utilizing a long pole made it possible to set the traps without wading in the mud which was of questionable depths.

    The next AM, at about the same time, the trapper again checked his trap line. The tide was coming in and he decided to wade out into the ditch and take the captive muskrats from the traps that he had set the night before. Shining his flashlight into the ditch, He could see two large black muskrats caught in the traps. Black muskrats could be sold for several dollars more than the normally brown muskrats. Nothing is wasted when trapping muskrats. The pelts were sold to fur buyers and the meat sold for human consumption. Muskrats aren't really *rats* but are a member of the rodent family. In Delaware muskrats are considered a delicious meal for many people. It is almost a tradition in Delaware to enjoy muskrat meat during the winter season.

In the exhilaration engendered by seeing the black muskrats held firmly in the traps, he made the mistake of wading into the ditch to retrieve the newly caught muskrats. Once the muskrats were removed he would have to reset the traps and maybe move them to a different trail. He had taken less than six steps when he suddenly started sinking. In fright he begin thrashing in an effort to free himself. His near panic condition only cause him to sink deeper and solidly into the mud.

He had the presence of mind to lay down in the mud and cease struggling. Rolling his body into a swimming position allowed him to barely grasp several cattails growing near the edge of the ditch. Several pulled loose from the bank and he fell back into the water and mud. The incoming tide was raising the level of the water in the ditch. When he was finally able to grasp the reeds, he was completely under water except for his head. His chest waders were filled. The water was cold and shocked him to exert more effort to pull himself out of the deadly mud in which he found himself trapped.

Even with a firm hold on the cattails the man struggled for several minutes to free his body from the deadly grasping mud and quicksand. He was totally exhausted and covered with mud by the time he was able to crawl from the deadly grip of the mud. He was drenched with sweat from the exertion of freeing himself. Working alone can be fatal in some occupations. Because of his near death experience the trapper gained a healthy respect for the risks of trapping alone.

After that episode the man started to carry a canoe paddle when he checked his traps. He would test the mud with the paddle and if the mud was somewhat soft, he would kneel on the flat blade of the paddle. The paddle would support his weight and prevent him sinking into the mud.

CHAPTER 14

Meandering

In 1975-76 Weakfish were at an all time abundance in the Delaware Bay. Often forty to fifty boats could be observed anchored at the oyster beds. Most fishermen were confident of a satisfactory catch if they used the proper bait and were forbearing enough. Squid and peeler crabs were the favorite bait, while the bucktail lure was favored by many, especially during the early spring.

Often when the author motored to the oyster beds early in the morning, anchored and started fishing, other boats would start arriving and anchor near his boat. Once to see what would happen if he anchored just anywhere, he motored about three miles out in the bay and anchored. Soon other boats started arriving and anchoring near him. Apparently, people new to the bay assumed that an anchored boat was where the fish were biting. Another comical concept observed while fishing on the bay was that of people anchoring their boats miles out in the bay and then casting their lure as far as they could.

Wilson Carey of Leipsic, Delaware—several years deceased at the writing of this book—was a master fisherman. When the author would see Wilson's small fishing boat anchored anywhere in the bay he would anchor there too. Wilson was about the best fisherman the author had ever known during all the years fishing on the bay. The man fished commercially and sold fish from coolers and freezers in his garage in Leipsic. He had regular customers who always knew where to buy good quality fish at a decent price.

The master fisherman's mode of fishing wasn't much different from others. He would use two rods, one positioned in a holder attached to the boat and the other in his hands. If fish were to be caught, he would be the one catching them. People have fished along side Wilson and only caught one fish to his ten. The man possessed a special talent. He would almost make people angry because he was catching fish and they weren't. One season he caught 3,700 large Weakfish. He wasn't greedy, it was how he earned his living.

There is bad will between net fishermen and

Meandering

sports fishermen because the sports fishermen think the nets take too many fish from the bay. Taking so many fish by nets would give them fewer fish to catch with the rod and reel. In turn, the commercial fishermen feel that they have a right to earn their subsistence by following their occupation. They think that there is enough fish for both the net fishermen and the sports fishermen.

Once after pulling sixty crab pots by hand on an exceptionally hot day, the author was very thirsty because he had carelessly forgotten to bring a thermos of water. When working on the bay a person needs to consume plenty of water.

He recognized, some distance away, a small boat tied up to a fish net that had been left in the bay long past the netting season. The water was really too warm and any fish caught would easily spoil.

The boat's single occupant was a well known character who frequented Little Creek. He was still attempting to tend a net in the bay. Apparently, he would some times forget to check his net for days at a time. His was a situation that would make an avid sports fisherman angry. The net was filled with fish in various stages of decomposing. The man was attempting to locate a few freshly caught fish from his net so he could sell them to a market in Little Creek.

Many of the Weakfish caught in the net were over forty inches in length. The net must have been filled with several tons of the decaying fish. Anyway, the man tending his net gave the author a soda. The soda was perhaps the most enjoyable drink he can remember. He was that thirsty!

The author was upset about all the dead and dying fish trapped in the man's net. He didn't want to hurt the man's feelings and make him angry. He suggested to the man that the season was over, the water too warm, and "one of these sports fishermen might see your net and all these spoiled fish and report you to the Marine Police."

The net fisherman agreed, and said that he thought he would take his net up so someone wouldn't report him. Few commercial net fishermen would tolerate wasting of fish and would probably report some one breaking the law and wasting fish. Such acts of waste hurt all who fish in the bay.

The sports fishermen who fish the bay early in the season sometimes snag nets. This accident damages the net and cause considerable work by the sports fishermen to untangle the nylon webbing from their boat's propellers. On the other hand, the commercial fishermen become very upset because their nets are damaged. Perhaps they are thinking that maybe the sports fishermen aren't watching where they pilot their boats since the nets are clearly marked with floats. Both have a good argument on their different views. Indeed, there are many careless boaters fishing on the bay.

Many incidents occur on the bay each year. One boater was caught in a lightening storm a few years ago and a bolt of lightening struck as he reached for the motor to start it and head for home. He was killed instantly. It is a sad occasion when a person is enjoying the bay and disaster strikes. During a storm the boater is the tallest object around and a target for lightening. Watching the weather is a must for fishing on the bay.

Another boater was anchored at the oyster beds fishing. In the distance he observed a small dark cloud approaching his boat. When the cloud drew near he realized it was a huge swarm of bees. The boat's occupants watched in awe as the bees passed their boat, and then in concern, when the bees suddenly turned and landed on the console of the boat. The bees completely covered the console and controls of the boat. The people aboard the boat knew nothing about the behavior of bees except knowing that approaching their hives was a sure guarantee of being stung. They retreated to the prow of the boat wondering what to do. So far no one had been stung, and they surely didn't want to excite the bees and be the victim of that huge swarm.

The occupants of another boat anchored nearby noticed their predicament and call the Marine Police on their CB radio. The Marine Police located a bee keeper and gave him a ride to the boat containing the swarm of bees. Everyone watched as the bee keeper gently brushed the bees into a trash can he had brought with him. No one was stung, the bee keeper became the owner of a new hive of bees, both the Marine Police and the boat's occupants were relieved with not having to attempt removing the bees.

A man moved from Delaware and stored his 18' boat with a friend until he could sell the boat. The boat was stored under a tarp and after two years still hadn't sold. The owner called and told his friend that he should use the boat until a buyer could be found. That sounded like a good idea, so the man launched the boat at Port Mahon, Delaware. The man took his wife and three other persons with him for a fishing trip to the oyster beds.

The ride to the fishing area went well. It was a calm day and the water was smooth. The boat was duly anchored and hooks baited and tossed into the bay. Suddenly a wasp stung the boat operator. Then several other wasps attacked him and inflicted several stings. The boat was so small that there wasn't room to retreat out of the range of the angry wasps. The man killed several and then looked under the console and located four large wasp nests covered with wasp.

He grabbed a styrofoam cup and pressed the open area into each nest and then crushed the cup hoping to kill the wasps. The air was soon filled with angry wasps and the man attempting to evade being stung. Once all the wasp nests were in the water, he started the boat's motor and moved out from under the swarm of wasps. He was stung eight times and was feeling badly by the time he left the angry creatures behind. Thereafter, he always examined every crevice of the boat for wasp nests before towing it to the launch ramp.

Once a deer was sighted swimming in the bay a long way from shore. Several boat operators attempted to herd it toward shore. However, the deer was contrary and refused to swim the direction they wanted. The men wanted to save the deer's life. The direction the deer was swimming was further out in the bay. There was no way that they could envision the deer swimming all the way to New Jersey. Finally one of the men lassoed the deer and attempted to tow it behind the boat to shore. The deer only became wilder and soon expired from fright and exhaustion. This was a case of attempting to help an animal when it should have been left alone.

One enigma of the bay that the author observed was that of a large (five foot or longer) serpent swimming in the water three miles off shore. The snake was different from any snake the man had ever seen before. The snake was a light colored green. The author remembered seeing eighteen inch green snakes years before in the south. The green snakes there never grew any larger. Those green snakes where no larger in diameter than a large pencil. The green snake sighted in the bay was as large around as a coke bottle. He still wonders what species of snake he saw swimming in the bay.

Trapping has been an exciting occupation for many who worked the bay. There are certain risks involved in that occupation. One trapper was trapping from a canoe on a tidal stream. He had caught a raccoon in a foot trap. He tapped the raccoon over the head to give it a merciful death and placed it in his canoe. That tidal river is noted for deep mud and quicksand. At low tide there are few places to land a boat.

The trapper backed his canoe into the river and started paddling upstream with the intent of checking other traps. Suddenly, the "dead" raccoon came to life. Rather than jumping from the canoe and escaping, it jumped for the trapper. The animal was a large boar coon and it was mad. The coon was making a popping sound from opening and closing its jaws. The trapper slammed the canoe paddle across the raccoon's head. The coon because semiconscious in the bottom of the canoe three feet from the trapper. Meanwhile the trapper was striving to locate an area where he could reach land. Either the raccoon left the canoe or he would. There wasn't a greedy bone in his body. There was no way he was going to stay in a canoe with an angry raccoon bent on biting him. Two more times the raccoon awakened and attempted to attack him. And two more times he struck the raccoon over the head with the paddle. The last blow splintered the paddle blade.

Ahead of him was a point of land and he steered in that direction. When the canoe bumped onto the solid land he jumped from the canoe and pulled it up on solid ground. The raccoon came alive once more and started for him again. He reached into the front of the canoe and picked up a small hand axe he carried in the canoe and struck the coon a solid blow in the head. That blow killed the raccoon. The raccoon weighed over thirty pounds. That is a good size for a raccoon.

A trap line can be an exciting place. Once the author was trapping a large marsh that was bisected by several four foot deep ditches. On returning toward his pickup he had to cross four of these bisecting ditches. Each ditch was only five foot wide. Normally, he would leap across each

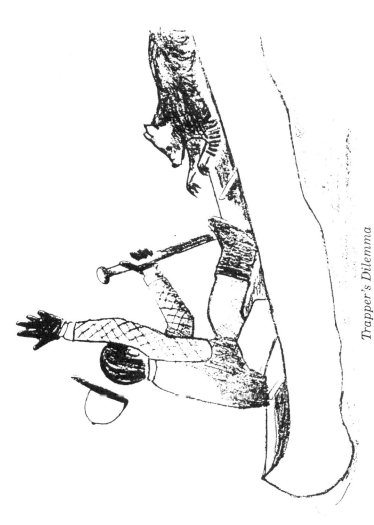

Trapper's Dilemma

What do you do when a very angry, teeth popping supposedly "dead" Raccoon suddenly comes to life when you are in a canoe with no place to go ashore because of mud flats and low tide?

Meandering

A Winter Swim

A local muskrat trapper's bum knee gives away at the wrong time. He was wading a tidal stream at 4:30 a.m. when his knee gave way. He fell backwards into the ice cold water. His partner later remarked that all he could see of the trapper was the beam of a flashlight shining through the water into the night sky.

ditch. When he leaped across the first ditch on the way back to the truck, a knee that he had previously injured gave out on him.

When the knee gave out, he collapsed on the wet ground. He attempted to stand and finally picked up a large stick that had drifted in with high tide and used that as a crutch to help get to his feet. The pain was intense and he still had three ditches to cross. He could expect no help because he was alone and no one knew where he was. Darkness would soon fall and being stranded in the marsh was unthinkable and it might be difficult to survive the cold night. The man looked around for a larger stick and discover a few feet away a twelve foot pole that had previously washed in with a high tide. He hobbled over to the pole and found it to be light enough to lift upright.

The stranded and injured man used the pole to vault over each ditch and land on his one good leg. He was surprised how easy it was to cross the ditches with the pole. When vaulting over the last ditch he fell flat on his face and lost the pole in the ditch. The fall didn't matter because he was near the truck and if necessary he could crawl the rest of the distance. He didn't have to crawl because he found another smaller pole and used that to aid him to the truck. The injured knee kept him out of the marsh for the balance of the season.